DALE ARE

Better Lucky Than Good

From Outlaw Biker to
Airline Pilot and Beyond

Copyright © 2021 by Dale Arenson Publishing LLC

All rights reserved.

No part of this publication can be reproduced, stored in, or introduced into a retrieval system, or transmitted in any form or by any means without prior written permission of the author or publisher.

ISBN-13: 979-8352389621

" 'Adventure' is a word people use to put a shine on lack of preparation and surviving through dumb luck."

~ **Jeffery Russel**

Contents

Introduction 1

Chapter 1 **Chaos, The Biker Lifestyle** 5

Chapter 2 **Alaska** 11

Chapter 3 **On the Wings of Eagles** 17

Chapter 4 **California Dreaming** 21

Chapter 5 **Back in Time** 27

Chapter 6 **The Trench** 37

Chapter 7 **Lost and Alone** 45

Chapter 8 **Mesilinka** 51

Chapter 9 **Fraser Canyon** 57

Chapter 10 **Mackenzie** 63

Chapter 11 **Hope** 73

Chapter 12 **Abbotsford** 77

Chapter 13 **On a Mission** 83

Chapter 14 **Smoke Gets in Your Eyes** 93

Chapter 15 **McCook** 101

Chapter 16 **Grand Island** 109

Chapter 17 **Jay Johnson** 115

Chapter 18 **More Determined Than Ever** 121

Chapter 19 **The Pilot's Pilot** 129

Chapter 20 **Like Joining the Circus** 137

Chapter 21 **Mistakes** 147

Chapter 22 **Flying on Pins and Needles** 155

Chapter 23 **Reading, Pennsylvania** 161

Epilogue **"This Too Shall Pass"** 165

Some Thoughts

Where are we going in life? The paths we follow… Are they the right way to go?

We never know until we try. And we never know until we've seen the results.

Do we take the safe path?

Or the dangerous path? You don't know it's dangerous until you've taken it.

The safe path leads to someplace obviously… safe.

The dangerous path leads to adventure and excitement. But it might also lead to an early grave.

I can relate only the paths I chose.

I had no road map. I blindly charged ahead and the best I can say is that I got lucky.

Introduction

"It's never too late to be what you might have been."
~ **Most often attributed to George Eliot,
AKA Mary Ann Evans**

This book is about success, which took time for me to achieve because it happened without the usual channels like college, trade schools, apprenticeships, etc.

"Better lucky than good," as my buddy and business partner Marc likes to say. It's an overly humble way of explaining his surviving a life of flying jets for the U.S. Navy and landing them on the pitching deck of an aircraft carrier.

It's also a way to explain success when you didn't have a plan or a goal early on. Of course, we all need goals, at least when we figure out what direction we're trying to go. I didn't have that for most of my early life. I was rudderless, drifting with the wind like a broken ship. The sails worked pretty well; the direction was another matter. That lack of direction took me into a few storms.

Then there's that saying, "Luck is where preparation meets opportunity." Some things might seem like luck, but if you're not in the right place at the right time, with the proper preparedness, that luck might fall on someone else.

Have you ever felt that you would have liked to have done something else in your life? But you thought you didn't have the knowledge, the talent, or the education? We tend to set limitations on what we can and cannot do.

Of course, there should be realistic limitations. If you were blind, you're probably not going to be an airline pilot. If you're six-feet, six-inches tall and two hundred plus pounds, you probably won't make it as a jockey.

But all too often, we limit ourselves and never try when we should be reaching for that brass ring despite what someone tells us – or, worse yet, what we tell ourselves.

The purpose of this book is to inspire others like me who didn't have the benefit of a good upbringing, a good education, money, or parental encouragement to know that they could do anything they wanted.

But there was the rub. In my case, I had no idea what I wanted. It took me a while to figure that out, and I got a late start. But, as they say, better late than never.

Most people have more talent and ability than they realize. In my opinion, there are only two things you need the most: a goal and the determination to pursue it.

In his book, "The Seven Laws of Spiritual Success," Deepak Chopra calls it intent and desire. If you have those two things, everything else will fall into place.

What would you like to do with your life? It doesn't matter how young or old you are. Especially if you live in America, the actual land of opportunity, all you need is that goal and determination.

Almost everyone wants more. I don't just mean more money, which is always nice and, yes, some endeavors can lead to that. Instead, I mean more challenge, more creativity, more happiness, and more success!

I'm not a life coach and I won't try to tell you how to do anything step by step.

What I will do, as an example, is tell you a little bit about my life and some of the successes I've had. There were also failures thrown in with things I accomplished despite my trying to get myself killed or thrown in prison when I was young.

You hear it all the time: "You can do it!" Well, I genuinely believe that, based on the results in my life. The funny part is, I stumbled through life and succeeded anyway. I want to share that story with you.

If I can do it, you can do it.

Chapter 1
Chaos, The Biker Lifestyle

"Get your motor running, head out on the highway."

~ **Steppenwolf**

Late at night on Route 66, heading eastbound through the Texas Panhandle, I was riding with a dozen other members of my motorcycle club, the Hangmen. It was the summer of 1974 and the heat that we had been riding in all day while mounted on our radical custom choppers had given way to a perfect temperature of 70 degrees.

We were part of the "So.Cal." chapter of the club, heading to Oklahoma City to meet up with the "OKLA" guys and party it up for a week.

The night before, we'd camped in Albuquerque at the house of a stranger whom we'd "kidnapped" at a convenience store. The first day was mostly desert and heat, then rain.

The second day wasn't as bad. When the sun went down, it was a pleasant ride. Being only two hours from our destination, we started to crank on those throttles harder and harder.

Feeling the thrill of speed and feeding off each other's daring and recklessness, we were soon holding the throttles on our geared-up Harleys wide open, grinning and shouting at each other over the noise for the sheer fun of it.

Flashing chrome with our long front forks, skinny front wheels, sissy bars, and roaring exhaust pipes. Stomping on suicide clutches and grabbing gears.

Clean, shiny bikes ridden by dirty, long-haired, and bearded rebels. We were no strangers to breaking the law. The trick was not getting caught. Sometimes it worked, sometimes it didn't.

With no speedometers, we didn't know how fast we were going, but it was at least 120 miles per hour.

It was late, probably midnight, and there was almost no traffic on the road when we roared through the small town of Shamrock, Texas. We did slow down a bit, doing maybe 50 through a 25-mile-per-hour zone, but we still probably woke people up, rattling their windows with our loud pipes as we blasted through town.

This was before the completion of Interstate 40. There were very few bypasses and we would most often ride through the middle of towns on Route 66.

After Shamrock, we picked up the pace to where we were once again holding the bikes wide open. This kind of riding uses gas quickly, and our gas tanks were rather small back then because it was more important to look cool than to have increased range. Comfort wasn't an issue either, as we were young and tough. This wasn't a hobby; it was our life every day of the year.

Having been "getting on it" for almost an hour, our leaders knew we'd be needing gas.

Past our windblown eyes flashed a sign that said, "Oklahoma State Line." Just past that, a neon glow gave way to the image of an all-night gas station.

Waving his arm downward to slow the speeding pack, Tom, our leader, started braking hard. After some screeching and squealing of tires, he got us under control. Shortly, we were lining up at a set of gas pumps under harsh neon lights.

Laughing and talking about the fun ride, guys climbed off their bikes, lit cigarettes, and threw off their leather jackets while others started filling their tanks. There was a diner that was open all night; a couple of guys wandered in there and grabbed stools at the counter.

A club brother named Curt asked me, "How fast do you think we were going?"

I said, "I don't know, but I've never held this thing that wide open for that long. I was just hanging on to try to stay with the pack."

Curt laughed and said, "Yeah, me too."

Onto this scene suddenly appeared a police car speeding down the highway. When he saw the motorcycles, blue smoke poured from his tires as he hit the brakes and swerved into the gas station. When he pulled up and stopped, his motor was rattling and smoke started to billow up from under the hood.

He was a local town cop from Shamrock, Texas. We were now in Oklahoma.

Getting out and slamming his car door, he stalked toward us and started yelling.

"What do you think you're doing? You can't drive through my town like that!"

With a surprised look, Tom said, "What are you talking about?"

Still shouting, the cop said, "I've been chasing you all the way from Shamrock!"

Thinking fast, with a puzzled look, Tom replied, "We've been here for fifteen minutes… Oh, you must be talking about those guys who passed us. Man, they were really going fast. You better hurry up if you want to catch 'em."

Right then, another police car pulled in, also with the markings of the town of Shamrock. The motor on his car was smoking too. The officer jumped out, ran up to the first cop on the scene, and excitedly said, "How did you catch 'em? I was doing 120 and I couldn't even see 'em!"

Cop Number One glared at him and then glared back at us. We stood there shrugging our shoulders, hopelessly trying to look innocent behind our long hair and beards.

Knowing he was out of his jurisdiction, Cop Number One turned on his heel and stalked back to his car, telling the other officer, "Let's get the hell out of here."

He slammed the car door. His motor was still smoking as he peeled out of the parking lot with his deputy in tow, heading back to the Texas state line.

When we finished gassing up the bikes, we parked them in front of the all-night diner and went inside for a late dinner or an early breakfast. Sitting in booths together, we ordered food while marveling at the sight of millions of bugs swarming around the fluorescent lights of the gas station in the humid night.

Everyone had to tell their version of the high-speed run we'd just done. All of us got a laugh out of our good luck of escaping to another state and not getting speeding tickets.

Earl asked, "Hey, Tom, how much farther is Oklahoma City?"

Tom said, "About one hundred and fifty miles."

Curt said, "At this rate, it should take us an hour."

Everyone laughed.

The author in 1973, Southern California.

We had a great time partying in Oklahoma City for the next week. However, three of us, myself included, got arrested for "armed robbery" when an altercation happened at a bar called the Red Dog Saloon.

A guy pulled a gun and we took it away from him before he could use it. He pulled another one. While we were trying to get that gun from him, the police showed up.

After we spent a few days in jail, the situation got sorted out. They let us go, but kept him in jail.

These are just a few of the stories of my harrowing life as an outlaw biker. I detail it in more depth in my book, "HANGMEN, Riding With an Outlaw Motorcycle Club in the Old Days."

I lived that life every day for seven years. It wasn't exactly a life of success, other than successfully staying alive. If I'm to explain where I was able to go, first I must tell you about where I'd been.

Something about the sixties made life feel very temporary. I didn't expect to live to a ripe old age and I felt like I just didn't care. There was this nagging feeling that you weren't going to live very long anyway.

Perhaps it was growing up with "duck and cover" drills in schools and the constant specter of nuclear war hanging over our heads, which made life seem so impermanent.

Or maybe it was the Vietnam War, where the country was losing so many young men. Unless we were in college, we all expected to be drafted once we turned eighteen.

One of my solutions was to sign up with the Marines. But before I was old enough, a motorcycle accident and a broken back changed my priorities.

Not having finished high school, I had no chance at college. I didn't feel that I needed a higher education anyway. Certainly not for the life I was currently living. I had no idea what I wanted to do. A career? What was that?

I was having fun and life was adventurous. After living with the family I grew up in, I found that having a family of my own wasn't something I wanted.

Not having a family meant that I didn't have to support anyone but myself. All I needed at that time was my motorcycle and the clothes on my back.

When I did work, it was low-paying jobs, driving trucks or construction.

There were gang wars, shootouts, and more bar fights than I can remember. I was lucky to live through several motorcycle accidents, plus numerous run-ins with the law and some jail time.

Going to funerals – either for our guys or for friends in the clubs that we associated with – became common

In early 1975, at the ripe old age of twenty-three, I decided that if I wasn't dead by now, maybe, just maybe, I should start making plans for the future. A future I never expected or cared about having.

Chapter 2
Alaska

*"I can't change the direction of the wind,
but I can adjust my sails to reach my destination."*

~ **Unknown**

After seven years of that crazy lifestyle, I moved to Alaska, intending to get a job on the pipeline and make a ton of money.

That didn't happen because the unions in charge of hiring were based in the lower forty-eight states. They wouldn't hire locals and I wasn't in a union that did the work they required.

I got married to a pretty young lady. She had a seven-year-old daughter whom I adopted. We bought an old log cabin on an acre of land outside of Anchorage.

It had no plumbing or running water, but there was electricity and a wood stove for heat. It hadn't been lived in for at least twenty years.

December 1975. The cabin when we bought it, "as-is."

For years, I struggled to make money in construction jobs while my wife worked as a dental assistant and made good money.

All the while, I dreamed of learning to fly and becoming a bush pilot. I didn't have the money or the time to ride motorcycles, and in Alaska, in the months that were warm enough to ride, it was frequently raining.

To try to keep some adventure in my life, I went on hunting trips for big game, bears, moose, caribou, sheep, and goats, sometimes with friends, but often alone.

The trips were rarely successful, but there was plenty of danger, not just from the large critters, but mostly from the terrain and the weather.

I had found a way to risk my life again, and this time I wouldn't go to jail for it. As long as I survived.

But I wanted to fly.

Eventually, I worked my way from construction to sales. My father had always told me he wanted me to make a living without getting my hands dirty. I took that both literally and figuratively. That was always in the back of my mind.

I moved into a steady job in auto parts sales. Now that I had a steady income, we sold the cabin in the woods for a profit and bought a single-wide mobile home. With two bedrooms and an indoor bathroom, it was an absolute palace.

Finally feeling successful, I decided to fulfill my dream and start taking flying lessons. But my wife wasn't going for it. She thought it was a waste of money, just a replacement for my motorcycle. I told her that I thought I could make money at it.

That didn't matter to her.

Long story short, the marriage fell apart. We sold the single-wide palace and parted ways. I moved to a basement apartment in downtown Anchorage and she flew back to California with our daughter.

Three and a half years after moving to Alaska, I took my share of the sale of our property and started looking toward my new life.

I was on my own again. It had been a while, but I had spent a lot of time there in the past. I forced myself to move forward with my dream.

On one of my scouting missions at Merrill Field, I discovered a little two-seat airplane with a "for sale" sign in the window.

It was a 1946 Cessna 140 with a newly rebuilt motor and a bright, shiny, new blue and white Imron paint job. Just what I needed.

They wanted eight thousand dollars. I had enough for a down payment.

It was parked behind a small two-story building on the north side of the main runway. A sign on the front said, "Gordon's Flying Service."

Inside, the office had a counter with a glass front displaying books and pilot supplies. Pictures of airplanes were on one wall, while the other wall contained a huge map of the state of Alaska.

On one side of the room were small tables and chairs in front of a black board. It was, among other things, a flight school. An attractive blonde woman was behind the counter. She said, "Hello, I'm Neldina. What can I do for you?"

Before even introducing myself, I said, "I want to buy that Cessna 140, and I'll need someone to teach me to fly it."

A tall, handsome man with dark slicked-back hair, wearing a leather flight jacket and smoking a fragrant pipe, stood up from a desk behind the counter and walked over to me.

He smiled as he stuck out his hand and said, in a deep voice that hinted at Tennessee or Kentucky, "Hi, I'm George Jones, and you've come to the right place."

He reminded me of old pictures of Howard Hughes. I thought he looked like a pilot was supposed to look. He was the owner, operator, and flight instructor. Gordon was his middle name.

He said, "How would you like to go for a ride in it?"

I said, "Absolutely, I'd love to."

We walked out onto the flight line and he untied the ropes holding it down. It was so small and light, the wind could blow it away without too much trouble.

Telling me all about the airplane and explaining what he was doing, he did an exterior preflight check, a "walk-around."

He said, "Consider this your first lesson."

We climbed into the cockpit, which was so small, our shoulders touched. It made a Volkswagen Beetle look roomy.

He explained all the controls and what they did, then pointed out the gauges and dials and their functions.

George explained, "I'd let you take the left seat, which is the pilot's seat, but this airplane has brakes only on the left side. Until you get qualified in it, I'll need to be in the left seat."

This little old airplane was a "tail dragger." The two main wheels were up front and a tiny tail wheel was at the back of the airplane.

They are much more difficult to take off in and land than planes with more modern "tricycle"-type landing gear.

It takes extra skill even for qualified pilots. If you don't do it right on takeoff or landing, you can do a ground loop. That's a nice word for crashing.

[For all of you non-pilots, there is an aviation glossary at the back of the book to help you understand the endless acronyms of the flying world.]

Chapter 3
On the Wings of Eagles

"Whether you think you can, or think you can't, you're right."
~ Henry Ford

The little cockpit smelled like oil, gasoline, leather, and a hint of sweat. The scent of George's pipe tobacco was somehow comforting.

When he fired up the four-cylinder, eighty-five horsepower Lycoming engine, it roared to life. Then he pulled back the throttle. It idled smoothly, happy to be running again.

Using the little one-hundred-channel comm radio, the only radio in the airplane, George called the tower and got instructions for taxi and takeoff.

My pulse was pounding. It was more exciting than riding a Harley chopper with the police chasing you!

Everything seemed to happen very quickly. After lifting off from runway 25, he surprised me by telling me to take the controls.

"What? Are you sure?"

"Of course. You want to be a pilot, don't you? Just do what I tell you and everything will be fine." His voice was soothing and confident, which helped me to relax. Suddenly, there I was, flying an airplane. It was magical.

Normally, I would have been looking out the window, enjoying the view from the air, but I was totally focused, immersed in doing everything he said: "Watch the horizon, pull the throttle back a little, set twenty-three hundred RPMs, this gauge right here.

"Bank right, add a little bit of right rudder, easy… not too much, watch the ball, now level the wings, just a touch of left rudder, and watch your altitude, try to hold it at three thousand feet." I loved every second of it.

Back on the ground, I was sold and got the information I needed on the Cessna. I was lucky to not get any speeding tickets while driving to the bank for a loan. When I left, I told George and Neldina, "I'll be back."

Flying was something I "knew" I could do. I could ride a motorcycle and I felt that an airplane was the same, just with a different dimension of vertical added in.

There were only two things that I thought might stop me. One was motion sickness. When I was a kid, I had frequently gotten sick in cars. Having ridden in small airplanes a few times, I had felt that awful sensation again.

The other possible barrier was math. I hadn't done well in school and thought I was bad with numbers. Manipulating the controls of an airplane was one thing; the thought of having to do mathematical calculations, especially in the cockpit of an airplane, scared me. But I pressed on anyway. I had to know if I could do it.

Once the deal was done, I owned an airplane and was ready to start my lessons. I felt like I had already come a long way.

I plunged headlong into the training, not just the actual flying, but also ground school. I'd have to pass a written test before I could take the flight test. When I wasn't at the airport, I was studying at home.

I had to learn aerodynamics, all kinds of navigation, weather, and how to read abbreviated codes for weather reports. Then there was flight planning for time, distance, and fuel.

There were also Federal Aviation Regulations (FARs) and all kinds of different airspace designations. It seemed bewildering at first.

After only five hours of instruction, George sent me off to solo. That was a lot less time than most students.

After that, I could go out and practice on my own, but there was still plenty he had to teach me.

I spent hour after hour flying cross country, either "dual" with an instructor or alone, and gained experience.

I learned rudimentary instrument flying, night flying, and every aspect of training George could throw at me.

Surprisingly, all the math I'd been so worried about came easily when I had something I enjoyed and could apply it to.

In just under two months, I passed my check ride and earned a private pilot's license.

I started to dream bigger. I wanted to make a living as a pilot. However, I had to learn everything I could, as a private pilot license wasn't enough.

To work as a pilot, I needed higher ratings: commercial ratings, instrument ratings, multi-engine ratings. They all took time and even more money.

Now qualified to carry passengers, I invited people to go up with me. To my surprise, they accepted. Wow, they were trusting! The sense of responsibility wasn't lost on me. It felt good.

Suddenly, it was winter again. It always seemed to come too quickly in Alaska. Now with short days and long nights, by the time I got off work and wanted to fly my plane, it was dark.

As a new pilot, you want to fly as much as possible. I was impatient to get more experience and start working on more advanced ratings.

The conditions in Alaska in the wintertime make that difficult. Trying to fly in the wintertime is a chore. The days are short and there are frequent snowstorms. It can take hours to prepare the airplane for flight.

Sometimes by the time you get it ready to fly, the sun has gone down, so if you still want to go, you must fly in the dark. Sometimes that's not so bad.

With a full moon, the ground is a pearlescent white contrasting with the black but starlit sky. It's almost a surreal dreamland, sometimes with northern lights dancing and shimmering.

In Alaska, it seems like nothing is ever normal or routine.

Chapter 4
California Dreaming

*"Imagination is everything,
it is the preview of life's coming attractions."*

~ Albert Einstein

Alaska flying in the wintertime.

After three and a half years, I hadn't been back to California, so I asked for some vacation time from my job and hopped on a Western Airlines Boeing 707 to Los Angeles for Christmas. It was 1978.

When I walked out of the airport terminal in L.A., the first thing I noticed was the perfect seventy-five-degree air. Then I noticed the palm trees. Suddenly, I wondered what I was doing in Alaska.

As I waited for the bus to Disneyland, which was the only public transportation to Orange County back then, I watched the cars go by. I was surprised at how old some of them were and how clean they all were.

In Alaska, cars don't last long, so you don't see a lot of old ones. When I say "old," I mean ten years. And in the winter, none of them are clean, as back then most people don't have garages. I never did. The roads always seemed to be a sloppy mess and automated car washes were non-existent.

When I arrived at Disneyland, my mother picked me up. I spent the night on her couch.

The next day, I went to a tiny airstrip in Huntington Beach, called Meadowlark Airport. There, I rented a Cessna 172, a single-engine four-seater, for several days.

This would be my base of operations for the next couple of weeks.

As soon as the checkout was complete, I took my mother for a ride. We cruised over the beaches toward Newport, then up and over the Santa Ana Mountains.

She was thrilled. Her youngest son was no longer a biker; he was now a pilot! Maybe he wouldn't spend the rest of his life in prison after all.

Flying the 172 in Southern California was amazing. Above the low layer of smog, the weather was perfect: clear skies with a few white clouds high overhead.

You could see mountains north and east, with the deep blue ocean to the west. With enough altitude, you could see to the south all the way to Mexico.

It seemed that there was almost as much traffic in the air over L.A. and Orange County as there was on the ground. But I was used to that, the area around Anchorage is one of the busiest airspaces in the country.

What was unsettling was that, below, it was solid houses, buildings, and busy streets and freeways.

In case of an engine failure, there was no place to put down the plane unless you could find a golf course or one of the big concrete riverbeds that take rainwater out to sea and are usually dry.

The runway at Meadowlark was only twenty-three hundred and thirty feet long and it was very narrow and surrounded by houses.

There was no control tower. Pilots talked to each other on a Unicom frequency to broadcast location and intentions.

Whether busy airspace or uncontrolled fields, even with my limited flight time, I was already used to them from flying in Alaska.

The next day, I flew the plane out to Hemet and landed at Ryan Field to visit some of my brothers in the Hangmen Motorcycle Club. It was nice to see them again.

A couple of days later, back at little Meadowlark, I happened upon a situation that was too good to pass up.

Taxiing the rented 172 away from the gas pumps after filling it up, I passed in front of a building that said "Sky Ad." In front was a big Stearman biplane alongside a slightly smaller low-wing open-cockpit monoplane. It had a World War II Army Air Corps trainer paint job.

The Stearman was bright and clean with white and red trim. All over it was writing that said, "Sky Ad" and "Bob Cannon." The other airplane looked old and faded, with patches on the fabric skin.

After tying down the plane in its parking spot, I walked into the little office and said, "What's the deal with that blue and yellow trainer out there? Is that a PT-19?"

A gentleman wearing a bomber jacket and looking every bit like a pilot got up from his wood and leather office chair, put his coffee cup on the desk, and stuck out his hand, saying, "Hi, I'm Bob Cannon."

As I felt his firm grip, he explained, "No, the PT-19 has an inline Ranger engine. That's a PT-23 with the Continental radial. The Army Air Corps used both for training during World War II."

I said, "Does it run?" It was almost Christmas and I was getting an idea.

Bob said, "Sure it runs. You want to fly it?"

"I'd love to. My father-in-law flew PT-19s while training for World War II before he flew B-24s over Germany. It would be great to take him up for a ride in that thing."

"Do you have any tail-dragger time? It can be a handful."

"I've got a couple hundred hours," I lied. "And I own a Cessna 140 in Alaska and I've been checked out in a couple of biplanes." That last part was true.

"Well, let's go then," Bob said.

Built in 1941, the plane was already ancient. In 1978 it was thirty-seven years old – ten years older than I was – and looked even older.

Only half of the instruments were in the panel, but it had an airspeed indicator, altimeter, wet compass, gas gauge, and oil pressure gauge.

There was no turn and slip and no vertical speed indicator, just holes in the panel where they were supposed to be. The control stick was a piece of metal pipe. It was everything you'd need for "seat of the pants" flying.

1941 Fairchild PT-23.

Bob put me in the front seat and he took the back. As we strapped into the parachute harness, he explained the idiosyncrasies of the old bird.

There was no radio, so we looked around the traffic pattern very carefully while taxiing out to the runway. We did an engine run-up.

The big Continental radial sounded wonderful, like a huge Harley-Davidson motor, only this one could fly. I hoped.

Pulling back the power, Bob yelled over the idling engine and the wind buffeting us from the propeller, "Pull on one notch of flaps, go to full power right away, the tail will come up quickly, lots of right rudder at first, keep it on the centerline, the main gear is pretty wide, and the runway is narrow, pull 'er off at sixty."

Like my little Cessna, the old airspeed indicator was still in miles per hour.

I nodded and gave him a thumbs-up.

When it was our turn, my left hand smoothly rolled the throttle forward to the stop. The engine thundered as we rumbled down the runway as if in slow motion. My feet danced on the rudder pedals to keep us straight.

I felt like I was in a time warp and had, gone back to the 1940s. It was mesmerizing.

At sixty miles per hour, I pulled back on the metal pipe and we lifted into the air. The plane flew like a big swan, nimble but lazy, with that big radial belching noise and sometimes a little fire from the short exhaust stacks.

At three hundred feet, I grabbed the lever, pushed the big button on top, and eased up the flaps. Bob had to yell at me to give instructions.

After only a mile, we turned down the beach at five hundred feet and flew over Huntington Beach. We did a little sightseeing as I got used to the feel of the old airplane.

Turning out over the ocean, I pulled back the throttle to test the slow speed flight characteristics and get the feel of the approach to stall.

Then, after some steep turns just for fun, we went back to Meadowlark Field for a series of touch-and-goes and full-stop landings.

After an hour and forty-two minutes of flight time and eight take-offs and landings, Bob declared me good to go, okay to solo in the old Fairchild PT-23.

Chapter 5
Back in Time

*"You can't go back to live in the past,
but sometimes you can visit there for a little while."*

~ **The Author**

The next day, December 22, my ex-wife Laurel and her mother Margret were in on the plan. We made an excuse to drag Earl, her dad, who was a former Army Air Corps B-24 pilot, to Meadowlark Airport.

The pretext was to have lunch because the café had the greatest hamburgers in California. Plus, there were airplanes.

After parking the car, we walked to the little café and chose one of the picnic tables in front near the phone booth. The lawn underneath had seen better days.

It was a later lunch than normal, but the other tables were occupied and for a Friday, the café was busy.

We ordered cheeseburgers, sodas, and iced tea while watching the occasional airplane take off, land, or taxi by. Cessnas, Pipers, here a Taylorcraft, there a Temco Swift. It was its own little community.

I shoveled down my burger faster than normal, then excused myself, saying I had to find the restroom. Instead, I disappeared behind a row of hangars.

Earl and the ladies waited patiently and made small talk as they watched airplanes come and go, enjoying the perfect day.

When Earl noticed an old World War II trainer coming toward them on a taxiway, he stood and walked toward the ramp.

He said, "I don't believe it. I used to fly one just like that in pilot school at the beginning of the war."

People at the other picnic tables took notice too, some pulling out cameras to snap photos.

When the airplane pulled up and stopped in front of the little café and Earl saw that I was behind the controls, wearing a Snoopy helmet and aviator sunglasses, he was speechless.

"What? How… What's he doing? Where did he get this? I don't believe it!" he kept saying.

As I sat in the cockpit with the motor running and that big propeller spinning, I waved for him to get in. Margaret and Laurel were laughing with delight, thoroughly enjoying the surprise.

The small crowd of spectators seemed to think it was pretty cool too.

Earl didn't hesitate. He fearlessly strode up to the plane and climbed onto the wing, then into the rear cockpit, where he put on the cloth helmet I handed him. He slipped into the parachute harness like he'd been doing it all along for the last thirty-five years.

Looking back, I realize that climbing into that old rattle-trap airplane with a pilot who had only one hundred hours under his belt wasn't a smart thing for him to do.

But he didn't think twice. Either he trusted me or he thought, 'If he can't fly this thing, I know I can.'

But then, I suppose it's the kind of courage you'd expect from someone who repeatedly risked his life in the skies over Germany during the war, flying the maximum twenty-five combat missions and surviving when many did not.

After pausing for a quick photo, we waved at the girls and rumbled off toward the end of runway one-nine.

When the final was clear, I pulled on one notch of flaps, swung onto the asphalt runway, and poured on the coals.

Lifting off, we floated upward and into the past. The sky is always the same, and it's always different. It's timeless.

Climbing into the hazy afternoon sky, we headed straight ahead toward the beach and the Pacific Ocean.

Open-cockpit airplanes reminded me of a flying motorcycle. You roar along with a big, throbbing engine, only instead of sitting astride it, you're inside it, though still subject to a fierce slipstream of wind. I felt right at home.

Crossing the shoreline, we headed out over the water and leveled off at three thousand feet. I spotted some oil tankers anchored offshore and had an idea.

Big and wide, they looked a lot like enemy aircraft carriers. In the interest of bringing back the flavor of World War II, I started doing shallow "dive bombing runs" on the enemy carriers.

Pulling out and crossing over the ships at about a hundred feet, we could see the crewmembers on the decks waving at us. We waved back.

After a couple of these on different ships (there were plenty of them), I twisted around and looked back to see that Earl had a big grin. So, leveling off, I shook the stick back and forth, the old signal for his turn to fly.

He understood immediately. When I felt him take control, I held up my hands so that he could see that the airplane was all his.

He gleefully made a couple more runs on the oil tankers, pulling up the nose to gain altitude after each one, then doing a wingover and heading for another one.

Soon, we were back on the shoreline at five hundred feet. We cruised along Huntington Beach, dodging the occasional seagull that ventured that high. A budding Jonathan Livingston Seagull, perhaps.

We could see the people on the beach looking up and pointing, with some waving.

The eighty-mile-per-hour breeze buffeted us as we flew, and the comforting rumble of the engine was reassuring.

On one side was the vast expanse of the deep blue Pacific Ocean, which seemed to go on forever. On the other was a vast, grey-brown population of humanity, which also seemed to go on forever. Crowds, traffic jams, pollution.

And here we were, just the two of us, lost in our own thoughts, lost in our own little world, lost in a time warp in an ancient airplane.

Earl snapped this picture from the back cockpit.

As Earl flew, I was just a passenger and free to gaze where I wanted and let my thoughts wander.

A cloud cover was moving in, and the sun faded behind the clouds, The sound of the old radial motor thrummed rhythmically through the hollow fabric-covered fuselage. The roaring air was cool, but not cold.

As the sun got lower into the overcast, the sky turned to azure blue and molten gold in a rare postcard sunset without the ubiquitous smog.

An hour after take-off, Earl shook the stick, signaling me to take back the controls. I did a one-eighty, then turned inland for Meadowlark Airport.

Swinging around on final to that short twenty-three-hundred-foot runway, I pulled the lever to give us full landing flaps. Its length was more than enough for that big, slow, graceful swan of an airplane.

We touched down gently with plenty of room to spare and taxied back to the gas pumps where Laurel and Margret were waiting. Laurel was hopping up and down with her fists clenched in front of her like a little girl.

As I pulled the mixture to cut off and turned off the magnetos, the engine clicked over quietly and then was silent. At first, it was a little numbing as we climbed out of the old trainer.

I was pulled out of my reverie of visiting 1941 and brought back to the now. The present world of 1978 slowly came back into our consciousness. There were hugs all around. I think the girls were just happy to see us come back alive.

Still wearing the Snoopy helmet, Earl had a distant look in his watering eyes.

He said, "I never expected to experience anything like that. The last time I flew an airplane, people were trying to kill me, and I never cared if I ever got in a cockpit again."

With his voice choking, he continued, "But this… It was so peaceful and serene. What a wonderful flight. Thank you."

I was choking up a little bit too. All I could do was smile and say, "Merry Christmas."

After two wonderful weeks in warm, sunny California, during December, I was back in dark, cold Alaska. A plan for my future as a professional pilot was beginning to form.

Bush flying, as they called it in Alaska, was a big business. It was the aviation equivalent of driving a taxi or delivery truck, only more exciting and more dangerous. It seemed a sure career for me when I got qualified.

People lived all over the state in remote locations. For some, airplanes were the only way in and out. Then there were the sportsmen who wanted to be dropped off for fishing and hunting trips, sometimes with guides, sometimes by themselves with their camping gear, usually in groups of two or more.

Flying in Alaska was always an adventure. Some of the pioneer bush pilots in the state had become legendary for their exploits in the Last Frontier. I wanted to be one of them. Maybe because of my background, lack of formal education, a habit of risk taking and overall rebel attitude, I felt that I had a shot.

Landing on a rocky beach at Kachemak Bay to dig for clams.

First, I needed a commercial pilot's license. Two hundred and fifty hours of flight time was needed, plus special training and, as with all pilot ratings, an additional written test.

There are flight schools and aviation universities that provide all aspects of training for future commercial and even airline pilots. However, like any education, they cost a lot of money.

I never even considered that route. I decided to go it alone and pay as I went. However, up north, it seemed like it would take twice as long due to the harsh conditions. Plus, everything costs more in Alaska.

After my brief respite from the Alaskan winter, the call of Southern California was strong. As soon as I returned home and to my auto parts job, I started making plans to leave. In the meantime, I needed to build up flight hours, so I flew my little airplane whenever I could, to wherever I could.

My plan was to "go south for a while, get qualified to work as a bush pilot, then come back and find a flying job."

To George, my flight instructor, I announced my intention to move back to California and to fly my airplane there.

He cautioned me that it could be a dangerous trip. However, being the adventurous type himself, he had flown the route numerous times and had confidence in my ability to do it.

Other people said I was crazy and that I would be sure to kill myself.

Which brings to mind a conversation from "The Empire Strikes Back":

Luke Skywalker:
"I'm not afraid."
Yoda:
"You will be!"

My sales job at Automotive Parts and Equipment Corp. had been successful. In the almost two years I was there, my accounts increased every month along with my commissions.

My sales manager and friend, Carm, was glad he had given me a chance and was sorry to see me go. I, too, was sorry to leave. He wrote letters of recommendation for future employers.

I sold what little I owned, including my car, and shipped my rifle and a shotgun to California. When the proposed time came, I said goodbye to the few friends I had.

After a buddy dropped me off at Merrill Field, I fired up my little Cessna and left behind the last four years of my life in Alaska.

I flew northeast to follow the Glennallen Highway to the Al-Can Highway at Tok Junction before turning southeast.

Bigger, faster airplanes might make this trip by flying down the coast in a more direct line. However, the weather next to the ocean could get bad and there were few towns and airports along the way. George gave me a lot of advice on what route to take and where to stop.

Also, a big factor was that my little airplane had no navigation gear whatsoever – not even an automatic direction-finding radio, or ADF.

The only way to determine which direction I was going was to use a little compass floating in liquid in the front windscreen. That, and looking out the window for landmarks: mountains, lakes, rivers, and towns.

That was why I was going the way I was, so that I could follow the highway. George said, "You can't get lost. There's only one highway between Anchorage and Vancouver, British Columbia."

I should have listened to him.

I was still a very new pilot, with only about one hundred hours' total time, when I left the civilization of the big city of Anchorage and headed off into the wilds of Alaska and then Canada.

High noon in Anchorage in December.

Chapter 6
The Trench

*"Always do sober what you said you'd do while drunk…
That will teach you to keep your mouth shut."*

~ Ernest Hemingway

Flying just above the treetops in my Cessna 140, I gripped the control yoke with sweaty palms and glanced nervously up at the right fuel gauge for the hundredth time in the last hour. It had stopped bouncing and was now sitting steadily on E… Empty!

I tried to control my breathing and noticed that my hands were shaking. I was in the middle of nowhere, waiting for the engine to start that sputtering and missing that it does when it's running out of gas.

It was a familiar sound, as I'd heard it not long ago, when I'd run the left tank dry to make sure I got every last bit of gas out of it.

But it wasn't just the sound that got you; it was the chill that ran through your whole body. This time it would be curtains, for the airplane and probably for me. It could be months, or years, before someone found the wreckage.

Shaking my head, I cursed my stupidity and carelessness for making amateur mistakes, but then again, I *was* an amateur, and probably should have heeded the warnings of people who'd said this trip was too dangerous for a new, inexperienced pilot.

Leaning forward, looking through the windshield, I searched for a sign of civilization, but there was none. Under my left wing was the one hundred-fifty-six-mile-long Williston Lake, pretty much in the middle of the province of British Columbia. On my right was nothing but trees and mountains.

There was no soft sand beach to land on. The thick forest came right to the shore of the lake. When the motor quit, I was trying to decide, "Do I crash into the trees? Or put the plane down in the water?" That would almost certainly cause it to flip upside down when the wheels touched.

I was going to crash! The only question was where and when.

This was May 9, 1979, and it was turning into a very long day. I'd left Anchorage for my trip south the day before.

After getting gas in Northway, Alaska, I crossed into Yukon Territory for another gas stop at Whitehorse. After seven and a half hours of flying, I slept in a tent under the wing of my airplane at Teslin.

Earlier that day, I'd had a peanut butter sandwich for breakfast and washed it down with water from my green plastic GI canteen. Once I was back in the air, I followed Highway 1, the Alaska-Canada Highway, to Watson Lake, where I gassed up and started my first series of mistakes for the day.

To save an extra day or possibly two, I was going to leave the safety of the Al-Can Highway and head off through the wilderness of the Rocky Mountain Trench.

It was a common route for pilots who wanted to save time and gas, as the highway heads east to Fort Nelson and Dawson Creek, hundreds of miles out of the way.

The trench is a fault line that stretches about one thousand miles through British Columbia and separates the Rocky Mountains on the east side from the Columbia Mountain range. It's such a prominent slash in the terrain that it can easily be seen from the orbiting International Space Station.

Flying into the unknown had the appeal of adventure, and there were gas stops in the trench; you just had to know where they were.

At the flight service station at Watson Lake, I asked the guy behind the counter, "Exactly where are the gas stops along the trench?"

He said, "Ingenika Point and Mackenzie. See that big map on the wall? They're marked on there. Just copy them onto your own sectionals."

"How far is Ingenika?"

"About two hundred and fifty miles. You should have no problem making it."

"Thanks. That should save me at least a day."

Then he said, "Just take a heading out of here of one-one-five degrees and you'll pick up the trench."

"Got it."

Walking to the wall, I found the spot marked "Ingenika" and copied the exact place on my map.

As I mentioned before, my airplane had been built in 1946 and the instrument panel was unchanged from when it was new. It had no navigation radios, just the communication or comm radio. My sole means of navigation was a paper map and the compass mounted above the instrument panel.

A modern navigation method is called IFR, meaning instrument flight rules. Mandated by the Federal Aviation Administration, it means flying by instruments only, in the clouds where you can't see anything out the window.

Airline pilots do this all the time. It takes a lot of training, and your airplane must be properly equipped, which is expensive.

Amateur pilots like me used to joke that we flew IFR, meaning "I follow roads."

But we – the little Cessna and I – were operating VFR, for visual flight rules. That means to know where you are and where you're going, and to keep the airplane right side up, you have to look out the window!

Google Earth now shows roads in the trench, but in 1979, other than a few logging roads, there were none. It was very remote.

Saying goodbye to the flight service guy, I hopped into my airplane and took off. Banking to the southeast, I made my first mistake.

Rolling out of my turn, I leveled the wings when I saw 15 on my compass, and off I went.

After an hour, while constantly checking my map for landmarks such as lakes, rivers, and mountains, I realized I was lost.

From the landmarks I could see, it eventually became clear where I was and what I'd done. Though I'd plotted a line on my map from Watson Lake to Ingenika, I hadn't written down the heading that the flight service guy had given me. That was correct, but I'd misinterpreted the compass.

Remembering the one and the five, when I saw the tiny 15 on the compass, I'd made the mistake of going on the wrong heading of one hundred and fifty degrees (150) instead of one hundred and fifteen degrees (115). A thirty-five-degree mistake. The longer you go on the wrong heading, the farther off course you are.

Second mistake: flying an hour in the wrong direction. I should have gone back to Watson Lake to top off my tanks, but I could go almost four hundred miles on full tanks, and it was only supposed to be two hundred and fifty.

Instead, I picked up a heading of 090 and continued until I started seeing landmarks that indicated I was in the trench. Now that I was in the right place, I picked up a heading of east-south-east.

Before long, I recognized the Kechika River and turned southeast to follow it.

Between the healthy purr of the engine, the clear skies and smooth air, and the lovely green mountains and blue lakes of British Columbia, I was getting lulled into a sense of complacency.

Except for my wrong heading, things were going much better than they had yesterday.

My mind drifted as I analyzed the situation I'd gotten myself into the day before, when I'd flown into a mountain pass where a rainstorm almost caused me to crash.

I'd found myself trapped between the clouds and the treetops when forward visibility dropped to zero and I could see only the road directly beneath me.

The mountainsides rising on either side prevented a U-turn, as I would have had to climb into the clouds. That wasn't possible in this airplane.

If I'd lost sight of the road, it would have been all over. Then I began to worry about power lines or a tunnel!

After about thirty terrifying seconds of holding my breath, I finally flew out the other side of the storm. Suddenly, I could see for miles.

All I could do was shake my head at my carelessness. It was a rookie mistake and I promised myself I would never make it again.

Now, following the Finlay River, which led me to the north end of Williston Lake, I was happy to have such an easy landmark to guide me. Before the two-hundred-and-fifty-mile mark, I passed over a dirt runway.

Looking down from three thousand feet, with just a couple of small shacks, I could see no parked airplanes and assumed this was a private field that didn't sell gas. It wasn't located in the same place where I'd copied Ingenika on my map.

I continued for another hour, pressing on toward the spot on my map. As I got close, I pulled back the throttle to save gas as I descended toward my destination.

When I arrived overhead, my mind started spinning; nothing was there. Either it had been marked wrong on the map at the flight service station or I had marked it wrong. Probably the latter.

My stomach was doing flip-flops as I realized that the gas I needed so badly was probably now behind me, way behind me, and I was in a very dangerous position.

I'd already run the left wing tank dry until the engine started to sputter and miss. Now I was looking worriedly at the right tank, which showed less than a third.

Mistake number three. Afraid to turn back to that airfield, I pressed ahead in the vain hope that I would find a place to land. I was pretty sure I couldn't make it back anyway, but maybe the airfield I needed was still ahead of me… Maybe.

Depending on maybes in aviation isn't a good idea.

Twenty minutes – and a lifetime – later, I was staring at the empty right tank. Now I was in the position I described at the beginning of this chapter.

After having descended to where I thought the airfield was, I wanted to climb higher so I could see further, but I was afraid to use more fuel. So, I was stuck at low altitude.

Other than pulling back the throttle and leaning the mixture as far as I dared, I had nothing left to do besides berate myself for another rookie mistake. I searched desperately for a place to put down the airplane safely when the engine quit, which was imminent.

A sandbar in the lake or a beach on the shore? A dirt road in the middle of nowhere? There were none. The trees came right to the waterline.

Calling for help on the radio would be meaningless. No one could put gas in that tank for me, and out there, no one could hear me anyway.

If I survived the crash and the radio still worked, I could use the emergency frequency and try to reach airliners flying high overhead, on their way to Anchorage perhaps.

They could relay a message, although I had only a vague idea of where I was. Besides, I think I was too embarrassed to tell anyone how stupid I'd been.

Following the shoreline of the lake at treetop level, I again looked to the right at the cursed fuel gauge over the right door. It was still pointing at empty.

The gauge, like the airplane, was thirty-three years old and obviously not very accurate, as the motor was still running. However, that wasn't going to last.

Suddenly, with no warning, through the right passenger window appeared what looked like a dirt airstrip, parallel to my direction of flight and just inside the shoreline.

It was only about one hundred yards away, practically right under me. For a second, I thought I was hallucinating. Was I just seeing what I wanted to see?

But no, an airplane was parked there too. Civilization!

Without worrying about wind direction, I pulled the nose up to get some altitude and slow down. Then I pulled on the carb heat and shoved the mixture and throttle in for the short climb.

At two hundred feet, the end of the runway zipped by as I leveled off and turned right for a close in base leg.

When I banked right, my heart almost stopped as the engine began sputtering due to lost fuel flow. The little plane slowed and started sinking toward the trees. However, as I briefly leveled the wings for a short base leg, the engine kicked in again.

Almost overshooting the line-up with the runway, I kicked in some rudder and banked the little taildragger hard right. This time, the engine stopped cold and it got very quiet, with just the ticking of the engine as the propeller windmilled.

Rolling out of the turn, now on final approach, I put down the nose to keep up my airspeed, trying not to stall, I was heading for the tops of the trees at the end of the runway.

I wasn't going to make it. I felt an odd sense of calm and sadness that I had come this far only to crash into the trees.

Within ten feet of the treetops, my eyes were glued to my airspeed indicator, milking the airspeed to keep from stalling the wing's lift, trading altitude for airspeed.

With the wings now level, some fuel gravity-fed itself back to the carburetor. The engine suddenly roared back to life.

The nose came up and I cleared the trees by no more than a few feet. I was so elated, I almost forgot to pull off the power to land on the short dirt strip.

As the main wheels rolled and bounced, I pulled back on the yoke to put down the tail and hit the brakes. On the ground, the airplane rumbled and rattled on the rough surface.

I felt like the luckiest person in the world. I tried to remember to keep control and bring it to a safe stop.

I slowed to no more than walking speed. The engine kept running as I taxied to the end and parked next to the airplane sitting there.

Pulling out the mixture knob and turning off the magnetos, I sat there in the numbing silence, not believing what had just happened. I realized that I was panting for air and my heart was pounding.

Finally, I came to my senses, opened the door, and unfolded myself from the tiny cockpit that had almost become my coffin.

I needed to find out where I'd come down to earth. Was I lucky to find this place? Or would I come to regret it?

Chapter 7
Lost and Alone

"I think we consider too much the luck of the early bird and not enough the bad luck of the early worm."

~ Franklin D. Roosevelt

On wobbly legs, I walked across the airstrip, looking in all directions. Nobody was in sight. There were no vehicles and no buildings. Except for the two airplanes sitting alongside the runway, it was completely deserted.

A two-track dirt road led from the north end of the airstrip, heading west into the trees. Walking over to the other airplane, I saw that it was a yellow and white Cessna 185. Up close, it looked brand new.

It was a larger, more powerful version of my airplane and it could hold six people instead of two.

I didn't try to open the door, but peeking through the window, I could see that the meter on the tachometer said it had been flown for only thirty-seven hours – enough for a few test flights and then a trip from the Cessna factory in Wichita, Kansas to where it sat now.

I took a deep breath and looked around at the deserted runway in the woods.

Why was the airfield here?

Why was this airplane here?

Where was the pilot?

Where did that road lead?

I had put myself in a position where I needed someone's help. I wasn't going anywhere until I got some gas.

I started up the road to find out who, or what, was out there. There must be a house, or maybe a village or small settlement.

It was late afternoon and the weather was still pleasant, but this was in the middle of nowhere in Canada, in May. It would be freezing at night.

I wasn't worried, as my tent and down sleeping bag would keep me alive. But my food was limited to a couple of cans of pork and beans. I could camp out here if I had to, but it wasn't my first choice.

The primitive road didn't look well used. After following it for two miles and finding nothing, I turned back.

I kept wondering; "Why is the airplane there?"

"Where is the pilot?"

"Was he out of gas too?"

"Did the plane break down and the pilot had someone pick him up while he left it there?"

"Did he fly in for some remote hunting trip, and he won't be back for weeks?"

"Maybe someone had stolen it and was going to take it to Mexico, but made a wrong turn."

I crossed my arms across my chest against the increasing chill in the air. I had left my jacket in the plane, but walking helped keep me warm as I consoled myself that at least I'd gotten some exercise after the four-mile hike for nothing.

A cloud cover had rolled in and it was getting darker. It looked like it might rain or even snow. I needed a solution soon.

Back at the runway, I climbed onto the wing strut of the 185, unscrewed the gas cap, and looked inside. The tanks were almost full. Obviously, he wasn't out of gas like I was.

A short search of the area produced an empty one-gallon plastic container for Prestone antifreeze. That would have to do.

Draining just a little gas from the sump drains on the 185, I put the lid on the container and shook it to clean out the antifreeze as well as possible. When I felt that it was sufficiently clean, I dumped it out and drained a whole gallon of gas from the wing tank. Then I ,walked over to my little Cessna and poured it into the right tank.

Repeating this process four more times, I ended up with five gallons in my right wing. It held twelve and a half. Twenty-five gallons total would have been a full load for me. The 185 carried three times as much fuel; it also used three times as much.

I wrote a note and wedged it and a twenty-dollar bill in his door, with apologies and many thanks. Even at five gallons per hour at approximately ninety miles per hour, I wouldn't get far, but my first order of business was to see where I was. I had to take a look around.

Firing up the little Continental C-85 engine, I marveled at its healthy purr now that it had sufficient gas.

As I taxied the wind seemed negligible, so I spun around to face down the runway the way I had come. Doing a quick run-up to check the magnetos, I gave her a pat on the instrument panel and said, "Good girl."

Then I pushed the throttle to the firewall and my feet started working the rudder pedals as I rolled down the runway. The feeling was like having died and then been reborn.

Ah, the little things in life! In this case, five gallons of gas.

Feeling flush with fuel, for a while anyway, I climbed to the base of the clouds at two thousand feet, pulled the lever to turn on some cabin heat. Turning to the west I searched the hills and forest. There had to be more here than just one little airstrip.

To the west rose the lowlands of the Columbia mountain range. Everywhere I looked were rolling hills full of pine trees, with a myriad of creeks feeding into Williston Lake. It was beautiful country, except, if you really didn't want to be there, the beauty was subjective.

I planned to do a short recon, not using too much gas. If I didn't find anything, I'd head back to that little airstrip and land before it got dark because I had no landing light.

I'd set up my tent, settle in, and wait to see what happened. Hopefully, my beans would hold out for a couple of days, and I wouldn't still be there when winter set in again. My .22 survival rifle was a bit light for moose.

Turning west and a little north, I had to drop in altitude because the fast-moving cloud layer was getting lower. Soon, I was down to one thousand feet, just skimming over a ridge within feet of the trees to stay under the clouds.

I had just decided to turn back when I spotted another runway. After I cleared the ridge, it appeared right under me.

As I flew over it, I noticed several cabins and buildings. A town or village: real civilization! My spirit soared. It was like a reprieve from a death sentence.

At least, that was how it felt at the time. My luck was really holding today, despite my carelessness and inexperience.

As I pulled back the power and turned onto a left downwind leg to land, I noticed a pickup truck racing down a dirt road toward the runway with a plume of dust trailing behind it. A welcoming committee!

Turning final I floated down onto this new runway. It was still dirt, but bigger, wider, and smoother than the other one. I felt like I was landing at JFK.

The pickup truck I'd seen was waiting for me at the far end, parked off to the side, so I taxied toward it.

Getting out of his truck, the driver pointed to a spot between two large tree trunks laying on the ground. I saw that they had tie-down ropes for an airplane, so I pulled in there and shut down.

Except for this one beat-up pickup truck, the place looked deserted. There were no other vehicles, and the buildings were boarded up. It looked like a ghost town.

I grabbed my jacket from behind the seat and opened the door. Compared to the other little airstrip, I felt overjoyed to have found this place. I couldn't have done better if I'd known what I was doing.

The man walked up to my plane as I got out. He had salt and pepper hair and a mustache and was seemingly impervious to the dropping temperature. He wore only a loose-fitting sweater. He wasn't smiling.

His first words were, "You're not the mail plane!"

Pulling on my jacket, I said, "No… Is this Ingenika?"

He said, "No, this is Mesilinka."

"Where's Ingenika?"

"I have no idea, never heard of it."

"Do you have gas?"

"There may be some in these barrels for the mail plane. We can probably scrounge you a few gallons in the morning. But you're not going anywhere today. It's too late and there's some weather moving in. You'll have to spend the night."

"That's fine, I have a tent."

He said, "No, you have to come up to my house. You can stay there. My daughters are making dinner. They'll be excited to see you."

I thought, 'This can't be happening.'

He wouldn't take no for an answer, not that it ever entered my mind. He said, "C'mon, let's tie down your airplane and drive on up. They're making spaghetti tonight."

I tried to dismiss my visions of the old traveling salesman jokes about the farmer and his daughters.

Chapter 8
Mesilinka

> "...luck is not to be coerced."
> ~ Albert Camus

The Mesilinka airstrip.

Sitting in the old pickup, rumbling up the well-maintained dirt roads, we climbed in elevation into the forest, away from the airstrip and the deserted buildings.

I wondered what I'd gotten into. It felt like some weird sixties movie, or was it the Bates Motel? Not long ago, I'd just wanted to get on the ground safely and would have paid any price to that end. Now, I was heading off into another unknown… What kind of price might I have to pay?

The cloud ceiling had dropped so quickly, we were now driving in a fog. My building apprehension was tempered by the relief that I didn't have to fly in this. Not being able to fly in the clouds, I might not have made it back to that little airstrip near the lake.

Maybe it was just the fatigue and stress of the day's flying. I was starting to feel disoriented and a little confused.

Half an hour earlier, I'd been worried about being stranded on an airstrip in the middle of nowhere. Now I was off to be the guest of honor in a situation that I had no control over, and I had no idea where I was, let alone where I was going.

My mind wandered. Would ritual sacrifices be involved? If so, I might have wished I'd just crashed into the trees.

There was a citizens band radio in the cab of the truck. The guy picked up the handset and spoke into it. "I'm on my way back. We have a visitor tonight."

Trying to stop my imagination from running wild, I asked, "What's your name?"

"Oh, sorry, I'm Matt. What's yours?"

"Dale."

"You'll have to forgive me. We've been stuck out here all winter, and other than the mail plane pilot, who never stays, you're the first visitor we've had in seven months."

'Visiting wasn't my intention,' I thought, but I didn't say it.

"Who's 'we'?" I asked.

"Just me and my girls. We're the winter caretakers for this place."

"And what is 'this place'?"

"It's the Mesilinka logging camp. In another month, it will be full of people and we'll fly home to Oregon."

As the foggy gloom closed in around us, he switched on the headlights and said once again, "My girls are going to be so excited to have a visitor."

I couldn't shake the feeling of being in some cheesy sixties horror movie, like "Queens of Evil." I tried to dismiss it as just fatigue and admonished myself to stop watching B-movies.

Before long, through the mist, the headlights revealed a dark two-story log home standing alone in the forest.

When Matt shut off the ignition and turned out the headlights, it got very dark. I kept glancing at him to check his body language, looking for clues that might tell me to run for it while I still could.

I was hanging back as we climbed the wooden steps to the dark porch when, suddenly, the porch light switched on and the front door flew open. There stood two little girls, literally jumping up and down in their glee at having a visitor.

I looked from them to Matt, who had a big smile on his face. "C'mon in," he said.

Both girls had bright smiling faces with blonde hair and blue eyes. The taller one was Mindy, ten years old, and the shorter one was Cindy, who was eight.

I relaxed and shook my head at my foolish paranoia. What was I thinking? Walking up onto the porch, I stepped inside.

The house was warm and smelled like an Italian restaurant. The dark wood of the logs contrasted with a stone fireplace where a fire was burning. There were pictures on the wall of wildlife like deer, elk, and ducks.

The girls were talking over each other, asking questions: "How long can you stay? Where are you from? Where are you going? Would you like to see our dolls?"

Matt said, "Take it, easy ladies, let him relax. We can talk over dinner. Now, how is that spaghetti coming?"

As they bounded off to the kitchen, Mindy called back, "Almost ready, Daddy."

Matt asked, "Would you like a beer?"

I said, "Sure, but I don't want to put you out or drink up your beer. I doubt there's a liquor store close by."

Heading to the kitchen, he said, "It's no problem. We'll be leaving soon and we need to use up our supplies before we go home. I haven't had anyone to help me drink the beer all winter."

Sitting at a dinner table in a warm dining room with a family, in front of a plate of hot spaghetti and a glass of cold beer, was surreal. I was amazed to find myself there instead of sitting at that lonely airstrip, waiting for someone to find me. I tried to pay attention and answer their questions.

I even had an odd thought that maybe I had actually killed myself today, and this was heaven. How many "Twilight Zone" episodes had I seen in which someone was dead and didn't know it?

I was pulled from my reverie when Matt said, "What brought you to our airport? Pilots flying the trench don't usually stop here."

Trying to keep my language clean for the girls, I said, "I messed up. I was supposed to stop at Ingenika Point, but somehow I missed it. I was lucky to find this place before I ran out of gas. You really saved my, uh, hide."

Matt said, "Well, good thing you beat the weather, cuz we're probably the only people within one hundred miles. I guess you got lucky."

"Man! You've got that right. So, do you have some gas I can buy?"

"There's no gas here for sale, but there may be a few gallons in the barrels near where you're parked. You're welcome to it. We'll check it out in the morning."

The spaghetti was great, and I complimented Mindy and Cindy on their expertise in the kitchen. They giggled and in unison said, "Thank you."

I didn't want to ask, but Matt filled in the blanks. With a sad look on his face, he said, "I'm afraid they've had to grow up a little faster than normal since we lost their mother a year and a half ago."

I said, "Oh no… What happened… if you don't mind my asking?"

"Not at all. It was a drunk driver. That's why we took this job here. Kinda wanted to get away from civilization for a while."

The girls stared at their plates. I just said, "I'm so sorry."

In a cheerier voice, Matt changed the subject and said, "Well, ladies, time to get the dishes done, and have you finished your homework?"

"Yes, Daddy."

They jumped out of their seats and went to work while Matt said, "How 'bout another beer?"

I was already half asleep from the first one, but I accepted.

As soon as the dishes were done, Mindy and Cindy were dragging me upstairs to see their room, with posters of Shaun Cassidy and Leif Garrett.

But the most important things to see were their Barbie dolls, complete with a house, a wardrobe, a car, and, of course, a Ken doll. It was all I could do to stay awake and act interested.

Matt finally rescued me by saying, "Okay, that's enough for tonight. It's bedtime. You'll get to see him tomorrow. Put your dolls away and say goodnight."

With a groan, they complied as Matt and I walked downstairs.

"We've got a guest room down here. I hope you'll be comfortable. Nobody has ever used it." Still not quite ready to pack it in, he said, "Now how about one more beer?"

I thanked him profusely and, trying to be a polite guest, agreed to one more.

As we sat in front of the fire holding the cold cans, Matt said, "You must have a lot of experience to make a trip like this."

I said, "Not really. I've been flying for only seven months and I have only about one hundred and fifty hours of flight time. This is my first long trip."

With raised eyebrows, he said, "You're either really brave or crazy."

Taking another swig of beer and staring into the fire, I said, "After today, I'm pretty sure it's the latter."

"You mentioned you're going all the way to Southern California. What for?"

"I've been living in Anchorage for the last four years. I'm moving back to California so I can work on my ratings to become a commercial pilot. Then I'll move back to Alaska and try to get a job as a bush pilot."

"Couldn't you do that in Alaska?"

"Sure, but down south, I can do it year 'round and it'll be cheaper to live there." I continued, "There's an airplane parked at that little airstrip over by the lake. Do you know anything about that?"

"No, I didn't even know there was an airstrip there."

The conversation drifted from flying to politics to UFOs. I endured long explanations about aliens and their mode of transportation. I told him how I envied the aliens, as they apparently didn't need gasoline, or even runways, and, unlike me, they always seemed to know where they were going.

Usually, a day has twenty-four hours, but after six and a half hours of flying and enough stress to last a lifetime, I was sure this one had at least seventy-two.

Instead of spending the night in a cold tent, I couldn't believe my good fortune and was never so glad to crawl into a clean, warm bed.

Sleep came like turning off a light switch.

Chapter 9
Fraser Canyon

"Life is governed by chance, not wisdom."
~ Robert Burton

I was in a forest of gnarly trees. Fog was all around and I couldn't see more than a few feet away. I didn't know where I was or where I was going.

Why was I here? I was lost and nobody knew where I was or where to look for me. This couldn't be heaven… Could it be…?

Then I realized that I was conscious. Confused, I wondered why I was warm and comfortable. I was supposed to be dead, lying in a forest in the wreckage of my airplane. Or maybe in my tent, starving and freezing to death.

I slowly opened my eyes to the smell of coffee and bacon, I was disoriented. Where the hell was I?

Slowly, my brain put together the previous day's events. Empty gas tanks, Matt, the girls, a cabin in the woods, the Mesilinka logging camp.

I looked around. The spare room I was in doubled as a storeroom for boxes of food and supplies.

It felt surreal as I pulled on a pair of socks and my jeans. Hearing voices, I opened the door and peeked out, then followed my ears and nose to the kitchen, where I was greeted by cheerful little-girl "good mornings" and a smile from Matt, who was sitting at the table.

He said, "You're just in time. Sit down. It doesn't look like you're going anywhere for a while. It snowed last night."

He seemed happy that I couldn't leave yet.

"You want to go bear hunting?"

Still rubbing sleep from my eyes, I said, "What?"

"There's been a big grizzly hanging around the camp. I saw his tracks just yesterday. We can get in the pickup and drive around to see if we can find him. How do you like your coffee?"

"Uh, black," I managed to mumble as I tried to get my head around this situation. "Bear hunting?"

"Yeah, a big grizzly. It would be cool to get a shot at him. You can't fly now anyway. The snow has almost stopped, but the clouds are still down on the trees. I heard on the CB radio that it's supposed to clear up later."

Mindy plopped two plates in front of us. They were loaded with scrambled eggs, bacon, and toast. Then I received a cup of hot black coffee.

"Wow! Do you always eat like this?"

"No, it's usually cereal, but I get tired of the powdered or canned milk. This is for our special guest."

"Well, thanks. Where do you get the eggs?"

"Sorry, but they're powdered too. Real eggs wouldn't last this long, and it gets a little cold here for chickens."

I took a big bite of the eggs and said, "This is great. I wouldn't have known if you hadn't told me."

Matt said, "Dig in! So, you want to go?"

"What, bear hunting? Sure. I haven't made any other plans for the day."

I was still amazed at my good fortune having landed me here. Going from danger and desperation to safety and comfort almost left me in a daze.

After we ate, I stopped by the spare room to pull on my boots and wool shirt, then grabbed my jacket and walked to the living room as Matt was pulling a rifle out of the closet.

It was a lever action with open sights and a heavy barrel. He said, "Forty-Five-Seventy, good bear medicine, at least up close."

I said, "Yup, that'll do the job. What bullet, four hundred grains?"

"Of course." Then, as he pulled open the door, he called over his shoulder to the girls, "You ladies hold down the fort and no playing outside because of that bear. We'll be back in a little bit."

There was only a couple of inches of snow on his truck. We cleared off the windshield and hood while he warmed up the vehicle with the heater on.

Matt chatted away as we drove in the gloomy light from the low overcast and thick, dark forest. It was still snowing, but very lightly.

Again, I couldn't shake that surrealistic feeling as we cruised the logging roads. I was supposed to be flying my airplane to California, but here I was in a pickup truck hunting for grizzly bears in the wilds of British Columbia with someone I had met only the evening before.

Matt said, "I've seen his tracks. He's got big feet. It'll be easy to see them if he's crossed the road. Then we can bail out and follow him."

I said, "Yup, it'll be as easy as following a sidewalk. I wish you had an extra rifle."

"Yeah, sorry, just this one."

After several hours of plowing through the soft snow in the pickup, enjoying the warm cabin, we spotted nothing: no tracks, no bears.

The cloud layer was thinning and we could now see patches of blue sky. Peering up through the trees, I said, "Maybe I can get out of here today after all."

"We hate to see you go, but I know you've got places to be. We'll head for the airstrip and see how it looks. That bear will have to wait."

By the time we pulled up to my airplane, the snow was already melting and sliding off the wings and fuselage.

Matt reached into the bed and pulled out a five-gallon G.I. gas can and a funnel. He carried them to some fifty-five-gallon barrels laying on their sides on the ground by the runway.

The barrels were almost empty, but he was able to get a gallon or so out of each one.

Ten minutes later, the can was filled and the barrels were empty. I climbed onto my wing and he handed me the heavy gas can. Using the funnel, I slowly poured the precious five more gallons into my right wing tank.

Tossing the empty can into the back of his truck, Matt squinted at the clouds and said, "This ceiling is still kinda low. We should go back to the house for lunch."

Glancing nervously at my watch, I said, "It's almost eleven thirty. I've got a long way to go today."

He said, "Just another half hour. You need to eat before you go anyway. That blue sky to the west will make for a safer flight."

I relented and we piled into the old truck again and headed back to the little house in the woods.

Cindy expertly sliced off pieces of canned ham while Mindy prepared the sandwiches and made another pot of coffee. I was amazed to find that the girls even baked the bread. Tom said they learned it from a book.

After what seemed like the best lunch I'd ever had, almost reluctantly, I said "goodbye" and "thank you" to the young ladies. Then, once again, we drove to the airstrip.

I climbed out of the truck and feeling hot, I peeled off my jacket, as the sun was now shining through a clear blue sky. Most of the thin layer of snow had melted from the airstrip.

Matt gave me an address in Oregon and, with a chuckle, said, "Send us a card to let us know if you make it to California alive."

I wondered if he knew something I didn't.

"I will. I can't thank you enough."

"Don't worry about it. It's been our pleasure. Well, you'd better get airborne. How far do you plan to get today?"

"First stop will be Mackenzie, then Hope. It's a grass strip down in the Fraser River Canyon."

Turning back toward his pickup, he waved over his shoulder and called, "Good luck!"

Chapter 10
Mackenzie

*"Let me not pray to be sheltered from dangers,
but to be fearless in facing them."*

~ Rabindranath Tagore

Having already untied the ropes, after a quick pre-flight check, I climbed into my little cockpit, closed the door, put on the seatbelt, and fired up the motor, which purred like it was happy to get going again.

I lined up on the runway, did a quick run-up to check the magnetos, and gave Matt a wave. Then I pushed the throttle all the way in and started kicking the rudder to keep us straight. In no time, we were airborne and starting a slow turn to the east toward Williston Lake.

On the way past the little airstrip I'd seen the day before, I looked down. The yellow and white Cessna 185 was gone. It was still a mystery as to why it had been there.

Climbing to thirty-five hundred feet, I could see clouds ahead from last night's snowstorm. They were moving southeast: the direction I was going.

Mackenzie, British Columbia was only about eighty miles away – it was a piece of cake to fly southeast down Williston Lake.

What a great feeling to be cruising along again. I didn't have a lot of gas, but it would do. The five gallons from that morning combined with what was left of what I'd gotten from the Cessna was enough to go the eighty miles.

I enjoyed the satisfying vibration of the purring motor and the clear smooth air, with the deep blue of the lake below me and green forests and snow-capped mountains to either side.

I was happy to be safely flying again. Life was good.

I mulled over my good fortune, not only to still be alive, but to have found some gas and a nice family in the middle of nowhere to take me in for the night. Talk about luck!

It reminded me of my old days of traveling on a motorcycle. The friendliness and generosity of people never ceased to amaze me.

After the last two days' mistakes, I felt confident that the rest of the trip would go as planned and that there would be no more crises, especially of my own making.

As I proceeded southeast, I came to an overcast of clouds that dropped lower and lower. I had to pull the power back and descend to twenty-five hundred feet. Before long, I was pulling the throttle back again, descending farther toward the lake.

Glancing nervously at the fuel gauge, I wondered if I should turn back to Mesilinka while I still could, but there was no more gas there.

And there were no other airstrips between there and Mackenzie.

Indecision… Press ahead or turn back. That can get pilots killed.

As I proceeded south, the shoreline on each side of Williston Lake got closer as the lake narrowed until it was little more than a river. I had descended under the cloud layer until I was just above the water, flying at about fifteen or twenty feet.

Now, in a narrow waterway, there were tall pine trees on both sides that rose to the base of the cloud layer. I had really done it this time, having put myself into a very dangerous situation.

I was flying in a tunnel with trees on the sides, clouds above, and water below. The sides of what was now a river closed in to about twenty yards on either side of my wingtips. Even if I had enough gas to get back to Mesilinka, it was impossible to do a one-hundred-and-eighty-degree turn to get out of there.

The clouds were just over my wings, and sitting on the tops of the trees made it equally impossible to go up. I was constantly being reminded that this airplane couldn't fly in the clouds.

Once again, I had gone from the frying pan to the fire. I started worrying about a bridge or power lines across the river which would force me to pull up into the murk. Unless I could go under it.

If I had to pull up into the clouds, we would almost certainly go out of control. Even if I had the necessary instruments, I would have to find my way back down, and if I wasn't directly over the river, I'd hit the trees.

Then there was the problem of structural icing that would build up on the wings and cause the airflow over the wing to stall. That meant I would crash. Even if I'd been able to fly in the clouds, that was a very real possibility.

Shaking my head at my carelessness again, I was angry with myself for getting into this. It was supposed to have been an easy day! How did I keep making these mistakes?

My mouth was dry and my breath was shallow as I tightly gripped the control yoke. My heart was pounding.

Fighting off a wave of panic, I forced myself to stay calm and concentrate on flying the airplane. My eyes strained to see as far as I could. I watched for obstacles and prayed that the visibility didn't go to zero.

I dared to glance up at the remaining fuel in the right tank. There was none in the left tank, and the right was fast approaching empty – just like yesterday, only now my situation was even worse.

I was trapped in a tunnel with no way out, leaving me no choice but to continue straight ahead. I was hurtling along at almost one hundred miles per hour and able to see only a few hundred yards ahead of me.

Once again, I pulled back the throttle and leaned the mixture, trying to make what little gas I had left last while slowing down so that things didn't happen quite so fast.

A couple of times the river widened out, but not enough for me to make a U-turn. I didn't have enough gas to go back anywhere anyway, so I pressed on as the banks closed back in on me again.

This bizarre situation lasted about fifteen minutes, but it seemed like hours before I started seeing small boats tied up alongside the river. Civilization! At least if I crashed here, someone would find the wreckage.

There were houses too, back in the trees. It had to be Mackenzie. My aviation chart showed that the airport was on the left side of the river, so, hugging the left bank, I eased the little plane as high toward the cloud layer as I dared while peeking over the treetops, desperately looking for the airport.

I saw nothing but a few cabins and more trees. I didn't know how far ahead the airport was – or had I already passed it? Another glance at the fuel gauge showed that it was now almost empty. Once more, I cursed myself.

The river had now widened out and was looking more like a lake again. I was still as close as I could get to the left shoreline, desperately hoping that an airport was somewhere around.

Finally, through the mist about a quarter of a mile away, I recognized a short control tower. I turned toward it, my wheels occasionally clipping the treetops as I got into the base of the clouds. I couldn't see straight ahead, only down, but it was enough to squeeze through.

Getting past the trees, I dropped back down and could see the tower again. My wheels were no more than ten feet off the ground. Luckily, there were no houses or power lines between us and the runway.

Grabbing my microphone, I called out on the Unicom frequency, "Mackenzie traffic, Cessna seven-seven-two-three-three, on a right base for runway one-seven."

A voice came back and said, "No other reported traffic two-three-three, you're cleared to land on one-seven. What are you doing flying on a day like this?"

I said, "Cleared to land one-seven. And, uh… It's a long story."

I widened out before turning final and kicked the right rudder and left aileron to skid into a right turn. I didn't want to bank the wings any more than I had to and have the motor quit like it had done the day before.

Rolling my wheels onto the paved runway, I breathed a huge sigh of relief and thought, 'I've been saved again.'

The voice on the radio said, "Need gas?"

I said, "Uh, yeah, kind of." I didn't want to admit the situation I'd gotten into.

He said, "I'll see you at the gas pumps."

Taxiing in, I started to think, 'This flying business is more dangerous than I thought. Maybe I'm not really cut out for it.'

I climbed out of the cockpit. Once again, it felt great to be back on solid ground. Being alive made me feel pretty good too.

My shirt was damp, and I shivered. I pulled out my jacket and put it on.

"Top it off?" asked the man in Carhartt coveralls.

"You bet, thanks."

"Where did you come from?"

"Mesilinka."

"Never heard of it. Is that north?"

"Yeah, about eighty miles, a logging camp."

"You're crazy flying in this. These aren't legal VFR minimums."

"It wasn't so bad until I got here," I lied.

"Which way you heading?"

"South, toward Prince George."

"Lucky for you, this weather is supposed to move east over the mountains. You should have smooth sailing in another couple of hours."

More to myself, I said, "I could use a little smooth sailing." Then, "Is there a coffee shop at the airport?"

"Nope, but I've got some coffee inside. Go on in and help yourself."

"Thanks. I've got some flight planning to do."

I sat at a table, enjoying the warmth of the office and the hot coffee. I couldn't help noticing that my hands were shaking a bit. Staring out the window, I could see little patches of blue sky.

The guy was right; it seemed to be clearing as the clouds moved to the east. I tried to relax and focus on the job at hand.

Unfolding and spreading my big World Aeronautical Chart (WAC) on a table, I started doing the math. My 140 held twenty-five gallons of gas, twenty-one usable. At four point eight gallons per hour, I could fly a maximum of four hours and twenty minutes.

At an average of ninety miles per hour, I should have a range of three hundred and ninety-three miles. But that was until the tanks were dry. I'd had enough of that kind of drama the last two days.

I didn't know how much I'd stretched those numbers the previous day and I didn't want to think about it. I just knew that I was going to play it carefully from now on.

The next big town was Prince George, but it was only about one hundred and ten miles – just over an hour in the air. I'd already gotten a late start because of the snow, overcast, and grizzly hunt that morning, so I wanted to make better time.

Instead, I decided that my next stop would be 108 Mile Ranch, about three hundred miles distance. That would give me an extra hour of fuel when I landed.

By dark, I should be able to make Hope, British Columbia, a big, wide grass strip along the Fraser River. After all the asphalt runways, gravel and dirt runways, and sandbars I'd landed on in Alaska, I was anxious to land on a grass airport and sleep under my wing again.

Hope was another two hundred and eighty-five miles from 108 Mile Ranch. It seemed conservative after the mistakes I'd made.

What I didn't consider was that five hundred eighty-five miles would take six hours, not including the time on the ground at 108 Mile to get gas. It was just past two o'clock and I needed to be on my way. By now, there was enough blue sky that it was safe to take off.

As I paid for the gas and said goodbye to the attendant, he looked at me kind of sadly, as one might look at a condemned man.

I fired up the little Cessna and blasted down runway one-seven into clear blue skies to the south.

Climbing straight out, I leveled off at five thousand five hundred feet and was soon following Highway 97 and flying the length of Mcleod Lake. Once again, I had full tanks, so I was able to enjoy the incredible scenery without fearing for my life.

It seemed like a quick three hours, passing over the large town of Prince George, then the smaller towns of Quesnel and Williams Lake. Soon, I was descending into 108 Mile Ranch and lining up on runway one-five.

After paying for my gas and using their restroom, a quick pre-flight and I cranked over the eighty-five horsepower Continental C-85 motor and was rewarded again as it surged to life and its steady idle.

She seemed as anxious to get going as I was. She trusted me, and I trusted her. Plus, she was grateful for the full tanks of gas I'd just given her. If she was happy, I was happy.

It was just after five o'clock. Only two hundred and eighty-five miles to go, and we would rest for the night on a grass runway. If no place to eat was available, a can of pork and beans cooked on my little gas stove and water from my G.I. canteen would be more than enough. My girl needed no food; she had gas.

An hour after leaving 108 Mile, I left Highway 97 at Clinton and picked up a southwest heading to the village of Pavilion. Highway 99 wove its way next to the Fraser River and I followed it until Lillooet.

Still over the Fraser River, the road alongside it was now Highway 12. Just south of that junction, I spotted a runway below me. This turned out to be Lillooet Airport.

As I turned south again, the sun had set below the coastal mountain range. The ground was still visible, but that wouldn't last. I hesitated. Should I land? I didn't need gas for a change.

The smart thing to do would be to drop into Lillooet, whether or not they had gas or food, and call it a night. But that kind of common sense always seemed to escape me.

I'd been in the air for only an hour and didn't want to lose the altitude. I had my heart set on Hope – very aptly named. It was only another hour and twenty minutes of flying time.

I passed Lillooet, which was another mistake that I would come to regret.

Soon, I was flying into the Fraser River Canyon. Then the overcast came in and the sun was about to drop below the horizon. I couldn't help the feeling of foreboding that came over me. I pressed on anyway.

At Lytton, the highway merged with Canadian Highway 1. It didn't matter which highway it was; I just needed to be able to see the river and the occasional headlights of cars on the road.

Flying in the canyon was a pleasure, at first. Well below the tops of the cliffs and the overcast clouds, the air was smooth.

Following the river and the Trans-Canada Highway was surrealistic as the orange evening light slanted in at an angle beneath the cloud layer. It briefly reflected off the blue and white mountains on the eastern side of the canyon.

Unfortunately, it turned into a nightmare.

As the overcast thickened and lowered, I descended into the canyon. It went from being patchy light from the sunset to pale blue and then to pitch black.

In daylight, I could have seen the base of the clouds. In the dark, they were invisible. I descended into the canyon to make sure I could see the highway and not accidentally fly into the overcast.

On both sides, solid rock rose to five thousand feet or more, a mile above the river.

The sides of the canyon were invisible in the darkness. I knew they were there, but I couldn't tell how close I was to them. I was flying in a tunnel again, only this time in the dark.

It wasn't as small as what I'd experienced earlier in the day, but because I couldn't see the canyon walls, it seemed like they were right next to me. The feeling was even more claustrophobic.

Outside my dimly lit cockpit, the only visibility came from lights from the odd home or building and headlights from cars on Highway 1. Everything else was inky black.

This little old airplane had no landing light, and the information I had said there were no runway lights.

My only hope was that I would be able to make out the airport as a dark area at the bend of the river, which I could occasionally see as a dim blue reflection at the bottom of the canyon.

Theoretically, there would be lights from houses and buildings around the airport. My aviation chart showed the airport to be just west of the little town, running almost due east and west, between the Fraser River and Highway 1.

I kept telling myself, "It should be a piece of cake to pick it out in the darkness. How did I get myself into this?"

Chapter 11
Hope

"Hope is the thing with feathers That perches in the soul…"
~ Emily Dickinson"

The little eighty-five-horsepower motor hummed comfortingly as I sat in the dark cockpit. Using the red lens on the built-in light so as not to affect my night vision, I checked the map over and over, looking for landmarks in the night below.

Having plotted the distance from Lillooet to Hope at ninety-four miles, I watched the clock, looking for the one-hour mark from my southbound turn.

Having drained the left tank, I shined the red light at the right fuel gauge to see that it was at half a tank. About six gallons left.

Cruising at only twenty-five hundred feet, I started seeing lights from the town of Hope. I started a descent, being careful to stay over the lights of cars on the highway.

Easing the throttle back in, I leveled at eleven hundred feet, which was a pattern altitude of one thousand feet above the airport.

Sure enough, just west of the town and between the river and the highway was a large, dark rectangular area. It had to be the airfield.

Already having flown six hours, I was tired, low on gas, and anxious to get on the ground. Over the small town, I turned west and lined up with the dark area, pulling back the throttle to start down.

Picking up the microphone, I called on the pilot-to-pilot frequency, advising that I was over Hope, landing to the west. There was no answer.

I had no idea which way the wind was blowing, but at almost four thousand feet in length, even a downwind landing should be no problem for my little taildragger.

Feeling a mix of elation and apprehension, I headed toward the black area ahead of me. I didn't want to put down in the dark, but once again I'd backed myself into a corner and felt that I was left with no choice.

At about one hundred feet of altitude, with my jaw firmly clenched, the occasional lights from houses passed beneath me. Suddenly, there was nothing but darkness below. I descended into the invisible void.

Trusting that I was over the runway, I pulled the power to idle and brought up the nose in a flare to slow down, waiting for the wheels to find the grass.

Peering over the cowling, silhouetted against the cloudy night sky, I was horrified to see the tops of trees rushing at me.

No time to analyze this situation. I shoved the throttle to the firewall. The little motor faithfully responded and, with barely enough flying speed, I pulled the nose up. We cleared the tops of those trees by inches.

Wanting to stay away from the invisible canyon walls, I immediately started a gentle right turn toward the river. As I gained just a few hundred feet of altitude, the blackness was closing in on me.

I flew with trembling hands, my mind in a whirl. What had I done wrong? Was that really the airport? As I cursed myself once again for getting into this fix, my tired mind sought a solution.

Then it hit me. I must have been landing downwind, with a much higher landing speed than normal. There had been no one to tell me the wind direction. "Yeah, that had to be it."

With that conviction, I decided to try it again, only from the other direction. In my haste, having gained only about four hundred feet in altitude, I banked the wings hard left to head back to the runway. Now over the river, having reversed course, I could see the lights of houses along the bank as I started to roll the wings level. However, the ailerons didn't respond. For a second, I was confused. Then the nose started to drop toward the water.

The airflow over the wing had stalled. We had stopped flying and were falling.

In the dark, at low altitude, in a stall, your instinct is to pull back on the controls to get the nose up. But that would only make the stall worse.

With a flash of sudden mental clarity, I remembered stories I had read about pilots crashing for that very reason.

Without knowing how close the dark river was, I knew that there was only one thing to do. With the throttle still at full power, I pushed the nose down, trying to gain flying speed.

As I did that, the wings started to level. My eyes were locked on the airspeed indicator. As it slowly and excruciatingly inched upward, I gingerly eased back on the control yoke. The little airplane responded. The nose came back up and the wings rolled level. The lights of the houses on the riverbank were now at eye level. I glanced at the altimeter to see it reading one hundred and thirty feet above sea level. My chart said that Hope airport was one hundred and twenty-eight feet.

I was within mere feet of the river. Pulling the nose up again, I started climbing. Once again, I turned west to follow the river and stay away from the invisible canyon wall.

I said to the airplane, "This is crazy. Let's get the hell out of here!"

I realized I was sweating, and my mouth was as parched as a desert. Shaking my head again at my stupidity, carelessness, and poor planning, I glanced up at the fuel gauge, which was now showing a quarter of a tank.

I had to find a lighted runway. Vancouver was one hundred and twenty miles away. I was sure I didn't have enough gas to get there, but once again, what choice did I have?

Chapter 12
Abbotsford

"When you're at the end of your rope, tie a knot and hold on."
~ **Theodore Roosevelt**

As I headed out into the dark night, almost out of gas again, for the first time I felt scared. It even seemed like the airplane was scared. She had trusted me, and I had let her down. She'd do anything for me, but she couldn't run without gas.

And now, for the third time in two days, I had put us in a position to run out of gas, and this one was the worst ever – at night!

In the other situations, I could have chosen a controlled crash, into trees or water. She wouldn't have survived, but I might have.

Now, crashing in the dark was sure to be the end for both of us.

I started apologizing to the little 140. She had been flying for thirty-three years and had finally found a pilot who would be her doom. I had made too many mistakes and was sure to destroy her. Even though I loved her. Isn't that how love works sometimes?

I reached behind the seat for my canteen, thinking, 'I'm not going to be able to talk on the radio if I don't get some water.'

Feeling my stomach flutter, I realized that I hadn't eaten anything since Matt had talked me into staying for lunch. That little interlude of safety and comfort suddenly seemed like light years in the past.

Vancouver was an hour away. I hadn't even flight-planned that far yet. Studying my aeronautical chart, I could see that my best bet was Abbotsford International Airport. It had not only a lighted runway, but also an all-night flight service station. If only the gas would hold out.

Climbing to only twenty-five hundred feet, I pulled back the power and the mixture to conserve fuel as much as possible as I followed the lights from cars on the highway.

After a while, I could see a wedge of lights shining through the canyon walls. They were getting brighter. The city of Vancouver.

I kept glancing nervously at the fuel gauge as it sank lower and lower. I tried to will it to stop moving.

Finally, I flew out of the black tunnel of the Fraser River Canyon and into a sea of lights that stretched from under one wing to the other.

It looked like Los Angeles!

I almost panicked. How was I going to find the airport in all these lights? But, with the fuel gauge now bouncing on empty, if the motor quit, it wouldn't matter whether or not I found the airport.

I knew from the day before that even though the gauge pointed to empty, the motor would keep running for a while. However, I didn't know how long that would be.

I scanned back and forth. The little cockpit was flooded with light as I looked in vain for the airport. I felt just as lost over all of these lights as I had in the dark.

Then I had an idea: a procedure my flight instructor George Jones had taught me.

I dialed the flight service station's frequency and pressed the mic button. "Abbotsford Flight Service, Cessna seven-seven-two-three-three."

I was thrilled when a voice said, "November seven-seven-two-three-three, this is Abbotsford."

"Cessna two-three-three requesting a DF steer."

DF stands for direction finding. When you transmit on their frequency, the station on the ground has a device not unlike an ADF in an airplane. It simply points a needle in the direction of the signal.

In this case, the flight service station can see your bearing from their location.

Abbotsford said, "Cessna two-three-three, transmit."

Holding down the mic button for five seconds as I'd been taught, then I read my call sign.

"Cessna two-three-three, we have you northeast. Turn left heading two-two-zero."

As I turned to two-twenty on the wet compass, I couldn't help but stare at the fuel gauge now sitting on empty and not moving. I prayed, "Just a little longer, please."

I was about to call them to ask if they still had me when he said, "Cessna two-three-three, transmit."

Holding down the button for five seconds, I said, "Two-three-three."

"Cessna two-three-three, turn left to one-eight-zero."

Peering at the little compass on the windshield, I rolled out on the heading.

"Cessna two-three-three, we have you in sight, airport is twelve o'clock, you're cleared to land runway one-nine."

I couldn't believe it! Right in front of me was a lighted runway on a big airport. I remembered to mutter, "Cleared to land on one-nine."

Pushing in the fuel mixture and pulling on the carb heat, then back on the throttle, I descended straight ahead and slowed to landing speed, then pulled the lever to put down landing flaps.

After seven hours of flying and drama, the wheels chirped onto the asphalt runway and I let out a huge sigh of relief. I felt like I was in a dream.

I was saved, again! I was alive. All the ugly scenarios of crashing that had been running through my head suddenly disappeared as I realized that my little airplane and I were going to be alright.

I slept under the wing on the asphalt of the transient parking area. It could have been a bed of nails for all I cared. I was just happy that my airplane and I were safely on the ground.

The next morning, the weather was clear as I hopped over to Bellingham, Washington to clear customs.

Back in the United States, my life got more civilized than it had been in the wilds of British Columbia.

Happily, there were no more harrowing stories, as I stopped making amateur mistakes.

The rest of the trip literally flew by, as airports with fuel were everywhere. The weather cooperated and I had no snowstorms or cloud layers to deal with. From now on, all of my stops were relatively short hops and I didn't need to fly at night.

I found myself flying over Interstate 5, passing over towns like Tacoma and Olympia and landmarks like Mount Rainier, the Columbia River, and Mount Shasta.

These were places where I had ridden on my motorcycle numerous times only nine years ago. I'd hardly known where I was going back then. It seemed a world away.

Finding my brother Neil in Puyallup, Washington. I hadn't seen him in years.

I stopped in towns like Puyallup to visit my brother, then on to Richland to see a pretty girl I used to know.

Once in California I landed in Redding to see my friends Jerry and Kathy who had left Alaska before me, then to Modesto to see Gentleman Jim. Just four years prior he and I had been riding and drinking together.

After three thousand five hundred miles and thirteen days on the road, or I should say, 'in the air,' I landed at the little airport in Huntington Beach, Meadowlark Field. The same place I had taken my father-in-law for a ride just six months prior.

Unfortunately Meadowlark isn't there anymore. The land was too valuable, it is now wall-to-wall homes.

Not having the time or money to further my flight training, I had to find other jobs to pay my bills while, agonizingly slowly, I built up more flight time. That was a lot easier to do in California.

I moved out to Hemet to be near my old buds from the club. I got a job as a warranty service manager with a motorhome manufacturer.

I had a steady income again. The sales manager was a private pilot and he hired me right away.

Some of my old buddies had bought airplanes and we flew together as much as possible.

I flew my 140 everywhere I could think of: to the air races at Mojave and Reno, or to any airport for lunch on the weekends.

It was a great way to get dates: offering to fly the ladies somewhere for lunch or dinner.

I was building flight time every chance I got.

I started working on getting a commercial rating, studying for the written test on my own in my spare time.

The sole focus of my life became my goal of being a commercial pilot. Everything I did was with that end in mind.

Chapter 13
On a Mission

"Here's the thing about luck...
you don't know if it's good or bad until you have some perspective."

~ Alice Hoffman,

October 1979. We were flying into a gloomy night sky with the lights of Las Vegas coming on behind our right wing and a soft orange glow off our left shoulder. We were apprehensive, already tired from a long day, and we had an even longer night ahead of us. Lurking ahead in that darkness were mountains and weather and the unknown. But we were on a mission.

Two hours earlier I had just gotten home from the motor home manufacturing plant where I worked in Hemet, California. It was Friday afternoon and the phone rang.

I recognized the voice of Tom, my old friend from the motorcycle club.

He said, "I just got word that my dad is dying. He's in the Mayo Clinic in Rochester, Minnesota."

"Damn, I'm so sorry to hear that."

"He's not expected to make it through the night. Can you meet me at the airport and we'll fly there?"

"Fly there? To Minnesota? In your plane? Tonight? I just worked an eight-hour day. What about the airlines?"

"There are no flights until tomorrow afternoon, and I'd have to connect through Chicago. By the time I get there, he may be gone."

Silently shaking my head, as I didn't want to spend my evening flying into the night to travel two-thirds of the way across the country, I said, "I'll be there in half an hour."

He had a 1949 Beechcraft Bonanza, a sleek V-tailed, low-wing airplane with retractable landing gear, but he had very little flight time and was still a student pilot. He needed me to fly with him to be safe and legal.

Having just surpassed three hundred hours of flight time, I wasn't yet a commercial pilot, but I was working on it.

I grabbed a jacket and my small flight bag, a toothbrush, then jumped in my car and headed to Ryan Field.

Tom was already waiting at his airplane. He said, "The pumps are closed here tonight. We'll have to get some gas along the way. Do you have charts to get to Minnesota?"

"No, we'll have to buy some. How much gas do you have?"

"About half full."

Doing some quick math in my head, I had to remember that this old airplane had an airspeed indicator in miles per hour, unlike knots in modern airplanes.

Thinking out loud, I said, "Okay, about twenty gallons. Las Vegas is about one hundred and ninety miles. Cruising at about a hundred and fifty miles per hour is about an hour and twenty-five minutes, at about nine gallons per hour. That's what? Twelve and a half gallons?"

Tom said, "Let's go!"

In no time, we were dodging airliners while descending into McCarran Airport in Las Vegas. As we entered the TCA (terminal control area), the commands from the air controllers came fast and furious, to one airplane after another. It was difficult to answer when they gave you an instruction.

Tom said, "Why do they have to talk so fast?"

They directed us to runway 01 Left and soon we were squeaking the wheels down onto the concrete.

After turning off the runway, we taxied toward the FBO (fixed base operator), Signature Flight Support. I called them to say that we needed fuel. Just as we parked and shut down the motor, a truck pulled up in front of us. Climbing out onto the right wing, I told him to top off both wing tanks with one hundred octane.

Walking inside, I went to the counter and asked, "Do you have sectional charts for sale?"

"Of course, which one do you need?"

"Enough to get to Minnesota."

"You're in luck. We have them for all over the United States."

We needed only four and Tom paid for them. It was his airplane and his mission. I had very little money, as I was working at a low-paying job and staying occasionally with temporary girlfriends or at my mother's rented single-wide trailer.

Looking out the window onto the ramp, we were impressed when we saw "Miss America," a P-51 Mustang owned by Howie Keefe, pull into a parking space right next to the Bonanza.

We were familiar with him and his airplane, as we'd seen him at the Mojave Air Races just a couple of months before.

When he came into the lobby, we said hello and made some small talk about his airplane and the air races while he waited for his gas. He was cordial and friendly. It was like rubbing elbows with a movie star.

Dinner was sodas and potato chips from vending machines. After we used their bathroom, the fueler came in with the bill and Tom paid for the gas.

With the new charts, and while munching on the snacks, I quickly plotted the next leg of our trip. Farmington, New Mexico was three hundred eighty-seven miles to the east.

At an easy cruising speed of one hundred seventy miles per hour, we'd be there in just over two hours. That would leave us with almost two hours of fuel to spare.

Within minutes, we had the Bonanza fired up and I steered with the rudder pedals on the short taxi out to runway 01L. The sun was just setting off to our left as we climbed over the city of Las Vegas. The lights of the city came on underneath the airplane. It was an awesome sight.

We were still low as we climbed straight ahead with Las Vegas Boulevard just under our left wing. The Vegas lights, along with the orange glow to the west, lit up the cockpit with a surreal effect. It seemed as unreal as Las Vegas itself.

Just five years prior, Tom and I had led a pack of a dozen outlaw choppers right through the middle of that town.

Leaving the city behind, we turned eastbound into a darkening sky, with the orange sunset reflecting off the waters of Lake Mead. Then we flew the length of the Grand Canyon. The sunset was at our backs and the golden light reflected off the eastern walls of the canyon.

Looking up, we could see the bright white contrails of jet airliners high above, still brightly lit by the setting sun.

Climbing toward the stars that were beginning to appear, we had to go to nine thousand five hundred feet to make sure we had adequate clearance over some of the mountains in northern Arizona. The terrain would continue to rise as we flew toward the continental divide.

Now flying in the dark, with the soft glow of the instrument panel, we were warm and comfortable, listening to the strong, purring hum of the one hundred eighty-five horsepower engine. We kept a heading of zero-seven-five until we finally picked up the VOR at Farmington airport.

The old A35 V-tailed Bonanzas had a weird cockpit setup with only one control yoke. It was either on one side or the other. If there were pilots in both seats, only one could fly at a time.

To transfer control of the airplane, you had to push a release button and then rotate the control column one hundred eighty degrees vertically to place it in front of the occupant of the other seat, so that he or she could manipulate the controls.

The control yoke itself would automatically stay upright.

Of course, both pilots had rudder controls, and each could manipulate the throttle, mixture, propeller pitch adjustment, and carb heat controls mounted in the middle of the instrument panel.

The landing gear and flaps were controlled by little "piano key" switches on either side of the throttle quadrant. They were within easy reach of either pilot.

However, there was only one set of flight instruments on the left side. That meant the person flying from the right seat had to look across the cockpit to see the necessary information on airspeed, altitude, heading, etc.

Doing that was normal for a flight instructor, though more difficult for a student. However, this wasn't a training flight. We were on an unusual mission, and the only objective was to get to Rochester, Minnesota… Preferably alive.

Most of the time, I would occupy the left seat, the PIC (pilot in command) position, and Tom would sit on the right.

Yet sometimes, so that he could get experience, I would have him sit on the left, and I would take the right. I was used to that, as I was learning to become a flight instructor, and flight instructors almost always flew from the right seat.

Tonight, I was in the left seat.

Approaching Farmington's Four Corners Regional Airport, we descended to six thousand five hundred feet above sea level. We were only one thousand feet above the ground.

Flying past the airport, because the wind was out of the west, we entered the traffic pattern, then turned back to the west to land on runway 25.

The wheels squeaked down happily; everything was going according to plan – even though we hadn't started with much of a plan.

We were relieved to find that gas was still available at ten thirty at night. When we topped off the tanks, another thirty-nine gallons total made our belly feel full. Or at least our collective bellies, as we felt at one with the airplane.

We headed inside to use their bathrooms to empty our bladders. Then we drank some stale coffee that was always available at FBOs. It's the same for both truck drivers and pilots: Stale coffee is better than no coffee.

However, the more coffee you have, the more bathrooms you need, so it's a balancing act. No food was available, not even vending machines.

I called the FAA flight service and got a weather briefing for our direction of flight.

Hanging up, I turned to Tom and said, "All airports between here and Rochester are forecast to be VFR. There's light rain and overcasts east of the Rockies, but no really low ceilings. The winds at ten thousand feet are forecast to be at least thirty to forty knots, about a forty-five-mile-per-hour push on the tail."

"How far will that take us?"

"That will give us a ground speed as high as two hundred and ten. Our max range should be almost nine hundred miles. We should easily be able to make Grand Island, Nebraska, then on to Rochester."

Tom said, "Sounds good, let's do it."

It was late in the evening and I tried not to think of what time it was at home. I'd been up at six and worked an eight-hour day, and I wasn't even sure of what time zone I was in.

In flying, you need to ignore the fatigue and get the job done.

The airport was deserted as we taxied out to runway 25 again. We turned into the wind and poured on the coals. I had Tom, in the right seat, make the takeoff. He did it like he'd been doing it all his life.

Just like riding a motorcycle, flying an airplane was easy. It was just all the other things you needed to learn that made it hard.

The takeoff roll was longer than normal at that high altitude, but the cool nighttime temperatures and headwind were our friends and we got into the air with no problem.

At five hundred feet above the airport elevation, we started a slow one-hundred-eighty-degree turn over town. Our goal for the night was to keep heading east and avoid those very dark and very hard mountains.

Tom said, "It's awfully dark out here. How do we know where the mountains are?"

"Stay over the lights of the cars on the highways. That will keep us away from the terrain. They don't build mountains over highways."

He looked at me sideways. "They don't build mountains at all."

"That was a joke." Then, for good measure, I said, "I hope there are no tunnels."

He said, "You're not helping…"

Climbing to fifteen thousand five hundred feet, the proper eastbound VFR altitude, we started picking up those nice tailwinds.

We had no ground speed read out, but could ask air traffic control. I could tell by my time/distance calculations that we were moving along nicely.

Making Grand Island would be no problem.

You shouldn't fly above ten thousand feet without oxygen, but we had none. We kept a close eye on each other for signs of hypoxia. It's a very insidious situation in which your brain gets starved of O2 and you start getting stupid and don't realize it. Fortunately, neither of us was a smoker.

Relaxing at our cruise altitude, we leveled off and enjoyed the tailwinds and smooth ride. There was no autopilot, so one of us always had to be on the controls.

Cocooned in our dark, warm capsule of a cockpit, we passed the time talking about the old days of motorcycle rides, fights, and parties.

What a strange transition, from motorcycles to airplanes. We were happy and life was good. But then it wasn't. Tom's father was dying, and we needed to get to Minnesota, tonight… Now.

He said, "If he dies before I get there, I'll never forgive myself."

I said, "You're doing the best you can."

Swept along eastbound with the tailwinds, we worried about the mountain peaks over southern Colorado. Many of them were over fourteen thousand feet, and we were only at eleven-five, so we followed Highway 160 through Pagosa Springs, Del Norte, and Alamosa.

It was a curving route that took longer than it should have, but it kept us away from those invisible peaks that would have put such a kink in our plans for the evening.

After Walsenburg, we left the Rocky Mountains behind. We could relax and dropped our altitude down to seven thousand five hundred feet. We didn't worry so much about hypoxia now, as we were back into thicker, more breathable air.

As we droned on into the night, fatigue crept in. The only things that helped us stay awake were conversation, navigating, and the occasional calls from air traffic control – usually just a frequency change to send us off to the next sector.

A thermos full of coffee might have been nice, but up there, with no truck stops to pull into, you don't want to descend out of those nice tailwinds to land somewhere just to get rid of the coffee.

We were happy to stay up in the thin air and tailwinds as long as we could. However, upon entering Kansas, we got some bad news; Kansas City Center told us there were cloud layers ahead. We needed to either go over the top or descend below the clouds to stay VFR, where we could see the ground.

We were not on an IFR flight plan, and it would have been foolish to go "on top" without knowing if we could get down through an overcast. That would have been bad enough during the day. In the dark, it would have been a nightmare.

I wasn't yet IFR-qualified, and the airplane wasn't IFR-capable. You had to have both.

We reluctantly accepted a clearance to descend to five thousand five hundred feet so that we could keep the ground in sight.

When we got there, we could see and hear rain on the windshield as we looked down upon the blurry image of middle America in the dark. Dim lights were scattered here and there. Farmhouses sat in the middle of nowhere and there were occasional headlights on a highway.

People were going about their normal lives on the surface of the earth. Meanwhile, oblivious to them, in the dark, stormy skies above, were two crazy people in the isolated world of a small, dark cockpit. They were picking their way through the unknown, trying to get somewhere they'd never been, to a place they didn't want to be.

The rain wasn't a problem, as the airplane needed to be washed anyway. But we had lost our tailwind, and we were depending on that to make it to Grand Island, Nebraska.

Our normal range would be a little over seven hundred fifty miles. However, we had pushed it to almost eight hundred. Now, without the help of that tailwind, we started to worry.

We were both tense: Tom because of his father and me because this was unknown territory – and not just literally. Flying across the Midwest, feeling my way at night in the rain, in an airplane that I wasn't very familiar with, was something I hadn't done before.

On the other hand, for better or worse, putting myself in dangerous situations seemed to be my specialty.

The radio was mostly quiet. It was about two o'clock in the morning and we'd been flying for over eight hours.

I stifled a yawn, trying not to think about how long I'd been awake since getting up for work the previous morning. But now was no time to try to take a nap.

Flying at this relatively low altitude, we repeatedly recalculated the fuel, time, and distance as we peered out into the night to confirm our position in relation to the map while crosschecking VOR radials.

Tom was flying from the right seat with the single-control yoke flipped over to his side.

Suddenly, a terrifying sense invaded our peaceful night flight.

I said, "Do you smell smoke?"

Chapter 14
Smoke Gets in Your Eyes

> *"I've seen fire and I've seen rain"*
> ~ James Taylor

Tom said, "I was hoping it was just me. What do you think it is?"

"I don't know. Oil pressure is normal, cylinder head temps are normal. It could be electrical."

We started putting our hands on the instrument panel, basically the only thing within reach. We moved them around, feeling for a heat source we could identify. The cockpit wasn't filling with smoke, but the acrid smell was getting stronger and our eyes started to sting and water.

We had no idea what could be causing it, but what we did know was… "This is not good!"

I said, "We've got to find an airport."

I had just grabbed the aeronautical chart when, suddenly, I felt a shock of adrenaline as the dark night was shattered when our forward view exploded with sparks hitting the windshield. It was like someone was shining a flashlight in our faces,

Instantly, Tom hit the release lever and swung the control yoke over to my side, saying, "Here, you take it!"

I was now wide awake!

Thinking that the engine was on fire, I pulled the throttle to idle, threw in some left rudder and aileron, and rolled the airplane almost onto its back. Then I dove it at the inky black ground below us. I had read about pilots putting out fires that way. Just as quickly, I realized my mistake; we weren't that high and I couldn't even see the ground.

Instantly, the airspeed indicator went into the yellow band, almost to the redline at two hundred miles per hour. The danger zone! Overspeeding an airplane can cause it to come apart. Immediately leveling the wings, I started pulling back on the yoke as hard as I dared.

That delicate V-tail wasn't as strong as a regular cruciform tail and there had been numerous Bonanza crashes in which the pilot pulled too hard and tore off the tail. That could ruin your whole day.

But being in a burning airplane was no picnic either.

With my eyes fixed on the altimeter, airspeed indicator, and artificial horizon, the nose came up all too slowly. I was trying desperately to remember the elevation above sea level of that invisible ground below us.

The wind was roaring outside the cockpit as the plane flew faster than it was supposed to. The good news was that no flames were licking at the windshield or coming out of the cowling. The spark show was almost gone.

Neither Tom nor I said a word. We were probably both holding our breaths as I tried to pull the airplane out of the dive.

Finally, the nose of the airplane came up to the horizon and the roaring noise subsided as the speed slowed well below our normal cruising speed of one hundred fifty miles per hour.

The few lights on the ground were clearer and brighter as we leveled at three thousand feet above sea level. We had lost twenty-five hundred feet, but it had seemed like more.

Our altitude was now only about five hundred feet above the ground. I started worrying about radio towers.

I eased in the throttle to maintain level flight. The airplane started shaking as if we were driving a car with a flat tire. Even with the power up, we started slowing down to one hundred twenty. I added more power and the shaking got worse.

Tom said, "What do you think is wrong?"

"I don't know, but at least the smell of smoke is gone, and I don't see any flames." Taking my map from where I'd dropped it, I handed it to him with my finger on our approximate location and said, "We're right about here. Find us a place to land."

He quickly found one. "Here's one at Norton, Kansas. It says the runway is twenty-three hundred feet long. That's awfully short. Take a heading of about due north."

We were able to hold one hundred ten as we shuddered to the northwest. When I tried to climb higher, the shaking got worse. Using the momentary toggle switch to adjust the pitch of the propeller to climb more efficiently didn't work.

We were stuck low and slow and decided to stay at three thousand.

Soon, through the misty night, we saw the green and white airport beacon that denoted a civilian airport. I made a slight course correction and headed for it.

As we rattled northwest, I tried to adjust the propeller again, but still got no response. Older and smaller airplanes have fixed-pitch propellers. It's like low or high gearing on a motorcycle; they're good for either takeoff or cruise, not both.

Modern airplanes that are more complex have a hydraulically controlled "constant speed" propeller in which you set the RPMs for maximum on takeoff. Then you choose an RPM for climb out or cruise. A governor keeps the RPMs that you set regardless of power changes by the throttle. It's the best of both worlds.

This airplane had an old electrically adjusted propeller. It was an early design and you had to manually adjust the pitch to get the RPMs you wanted. Every time you changed the power setting on the throttle, you'd have to adjust the RPM setting on the propeller. It was a primitive setup, but it worked… until it didn't.

Arriving over the airfield, I banked into a turn. When I looked down, I could see only one set of runway lights and they weren't very long. One side of the runway lights was out, and we didn't know which one.

There was no tower. It was an uncontrolled field with no one we could talk to.

By now, it was obvious that the propeller was stuck in course pitch. If we were cruising at one fifty, it was fine, although accelerating to that speed was another matter. For accelerating or climbing, it wasn't in the right position.

If we couldn't land on this runway and had to make a go-around, the airplane wouldn't want to climb.

Looking down at the runway, I said, "I'm not landing there."

Tom said, "We've got to. We don't know how long the engine will keep running."

I said, "As long as this thing is flying, I'm going to keep it flying. There's got to be someplace better than this."

Then I remembered the air traffic control flight following. Picking up the microphone, I said, "Kansas City Center, Bonanza eight-five-eight-one-alpha, we're having engine trouble. We need an airport with a long runway."

"Eight-one-alpha, your best bet is McCook, Nebraska, about thirty miles north. Can you make that?"

"I think so. Can you give me a heading?"

"Eight-one-alpha, turn heading three-zero-zero and dial in one-one-five point three and track it inbound. They have a six-thousand-four-hundred-foot runway."

"Roger that, thank you."

"Eight-five-eight-one-alpha, do you want to declare an emergency?"

"We're still not sure what's wrong. I'll let you know."

Center said, "Okay. There's no one at McCook this time of night and no emergency equipment. Would you like me to notify the local authorities in town?"

"Not yet. Let's see how this goes."

I rolled out on the heading and we chugged north into Nebraska, our seventh state for the night. I was beginning to worry about the motor mounts holding up to the vibration from the shuddering engine.

Losing an engine – literally, if it falls off – has a very negative effect on your weight and balance. It would cause the airplane to fall out of the sky, tail first.

Tom was looking at me like I was crazy. He said, "What are you doing? We have to get this thing on the ground, now!"

"I'll take the chance. As long as this thing wants to fly, I'm going to keep it that way." I'd learned to trust that the airplane would take care of me.

It was only thirty miles, but it seemed like a hundred as we struggled along a lot slower than normal. I suddenly realized that I was sweating, even though the temperature in the cockpit felt cold.

Following the VOR radial soon brought the green and white airport beacon in sight, along with the lights of the small town to the west. It was still raining as the runways came blurrily into sight.

Kansas City Center said, "Eight-one-alpha, wind is two-two-zero at one-eight, gusting to three-zero knots. Recommend runway two-two."

"Thanks, but I'm going to go for the longest runway. We're going to get only one shot at this."

"That's your choice. Give me a call when you get on the ground. Cleared to switch to Unicom frequency."

"Okay. If you don't hear from us in a little while, you might want to send someone to check."

"Roger that, good luck!"

"Thanks, adios."

We were still shaking along at five hundred feet above the ground, as if we were driving down a rough road. We passed the airport on the east side and entered a downwind pattern for runway one-two (one hundred and twenty degrees southeast).

The wind was eighty degrees off the runway heading, almost a direct crosswind, and gusting up to thirty knots, plus the runway was wet. This would be tricky. With the airplane unable to climb, we were committed to getting it right the first time.

Tom had relaxed a bit now that a runway was in sight. As we made a left turn onto a base leg, I called our position and intentions on the Unicom frequency, just in case any other aircraft were in the area. There was no answer as we flew the landing pattern much lower than normal.

With sweating palms, I turned onto the final approach. With the runway straight ahead, I eased back on the throttle and put out some flaps. The turbulence from the gusting winds got worse as we descended.

I fought to keep the wings level; the crosswind tried to push us off to the left of the runway. I kept banking the wings harder right and kicking in the left rudder to create a crab as we flew toward the runway at a forty-five-degree angle.

At about two hundred feet, I had Tom put down the landing gear. Thank God it worked. We got three green lights.

Now all I had to do was put this thing on the ground. I fought off fatigue and wished I could slug down a cup of coffee to get ready for the final test of the night… one way or the other.

At one hundred feet above the runway, I had Tom give me full flaps. I struggled to keep the airplane over the center line as it was pointed toward to lights on the right side of the runway.

I tried to kick in enough left rudder to get the nose pointed straight and lean the right wing down so we wouldn't drift off the left side.

Easing the throttle back to slow the airplane while lifting the nose into a flare, I tried to touch the right main wheel down first.

It was more like riding a bucking bronco than landing an airplane.

Tom said, "This isn't going to work. We should try the other runway."

I said, "We're committed. We can't climb to do that." I was beginning to think I'd made a big mistake.

After struggling one-third of the way down the runway, I got the nose pointed close to the centerline, chopped the power, and plopped all three wheels onto the wet runway.

The wind pulled the nose to the right as I pushed full left rudder and right aileron, trying to keep the airplane straight.

The wet runway worked in our favor, as we skidded like we were on ice. The nose was slewing from side to side. I fought the crosswind with flight controls while also using what little friction we got from the runway.

If the pavement had been dry, such a side-load on the landing gear might have caused it to collapsed. The wet runway saved us.

I focused on "flying" the airplane down the runway using the flight controls, interlocked rudder, and nose wheel steering. I didn't worry about using the brakes. The runway was so long that plenty of room was left.

When we got to the intersection of runways 4/22, we were slow enough for me to turn off onto a taxiway.

Tom said, "Wow, I can't believe you were able to do that!"

"That was a pretty bad crosswind. I really should have used runway two-two like you and the controller said. I'm just glad the gear held."

Remembering ATC, I dialed back to the center frequency, picked up the mic, and said, "Kansas City, eight-five-eight-one-alpha."

"Go ahead eight-one-alpha."

"We're on the ground at McCook. Please cancel flight following. Thanks for the help."

We both breathed a huge sigh of relief as we headed west on a taxiway toward a parking ramp in front of a large, well-lit hangar. Slowing to a stop in front of it, we saw a big, colorful neon sign over the large sliding doors. It said, "Beechcraft."

I said, "I wonder if this is what it looks like when you get to heaven."

After I shut down the engine and set the parking brake, we sat for a moment in the numbing silence. The plane rocked back and forth in the wind while raindrops tapped on the fuselage and windows.

Finally, Tom said, "I don't want to think about that. My dad is dying and now I'm not going to be able to make it there in time. This is the worst thing that could have happened."

"No, the worst thing is that we could be dead."

We popped the door open. The cold rain burst into the cockpit and instantly chilled us to the bone. I grabbed my jacket out of the backseat and climbed out behind him, onto the wing and down the step to the wet tarmac.

After almost nine hours of flying, it was two-thirty in the morning. Little did we know, the night was about to get longer and more interesting.

Chapter 15
McCook

"Remember that sometimes not getting what you want is a wonderful stroke of luck."

~ Dalai Lama XIV

Turning up our collars against the wind and rain, we walked around the wing to the front of the airplane, expecting to see smudges from smoke on the engine cowling. There were none.

Everything looked normal except that the propeller was stuck in a coarse pitch. As we opened the cowl latches to look inside, we were surprised to see the landing lights of an airplane on final approach to runway 22 – landing into the wind like I should have done.

I recognized it as a twin-engine Beechcraft Baron. What was it doing landing here in the middle of the night?

Tom said, "We need to find a phone booth and try to get a cab to a hotel. This rain sucks and we're not going to get out of here tonight."

The Baron turned off the runway and quickly taxied toward us. It parked right next to our Bonanza and five people climbed out.

When the pilot jumped down off the wing, he ran over to us, hunching his shoulders against the rain. He stuck out his hand and said, "Hi, I'm Jay Johnson. I run the FBO here. You guys need gas?"

Shaking his hand, I said, "No, we have engine problems. We were lucky to find this place."

"Yes, you were. I'll open the door and we'll pull it inside." Then he ran off toward the hangar.

Tom and I looked at each other in disbelief. Not only had we found a safe place to land, but we'd found a Beechcraft dealership, and the owner had shown up in the middle of the night.

The passengers looked kind of scruffy, like us. They unloaded their luggage from the Baron into a van that had showed up. They piled into it and were gone without a word.

Jay disappeared into the building through a normal-sized door. Then, with a loud electric motor whirring, one of the huge hangar doors started moving sideways, spilling bright neon lights onto the parking ramp.

Tom pulled his tow bar out of the luggage compartment and I leaned into the cockpit to release the parking brake. He was about to connect it to the nosewheel when Jay showed up with a motorized towbar and said, "Get inside out of the rain. I'll take care of this."

We watched from inside the hangar as he pulled first the Bonanza and then his Baron into the huge room and parked them.

Trotting past us, he said, "Come on into the office. I'm going to make some coffee."

Shaking his head, Tom said, "Man, this guy has a lot of energy for this time of night."

Once inside the office, we plopped down into some comfortable chairs. Jay said, "What are you guys doing out here this late?"

"Trying to get to Rochester, Minnesota. My dad is in the Mayo Clinic and they don't think he's going to make it through the night."

"Sorry to hear that. I lost my dad not long ago too."

Tom said, "Thanks, but now it doesn't look like we're going to make it there tonight."

"What's wrong with your Bonanza?"

Tom looked at me, so I answered. "Not sure. We started smelling smoke, then got a windshield full of sparks but no fire. Now the propeller is stuck in course pitch."

"Isn't that an old A35? Does it still have the electrically adjustable prop?"

"Yes."

"I think I know what it might be."

"That would be great… What are *you* doing out this late?"

"A charter flight. Those guys are a local rock band that just finished their gig in Kansas City."

I declined a cup of fresh coffee, hoping to be in a bed in a hotel soon and not wanting to be kept awake.

Jay seemed lost in thought for a minute, then said, "You're trying to get to Rochester tonight? Both of you?"

Tom said, "No, just me, but I don't know how we can do that now."

"I know there's a direct flight from Grand Island every morning to Minneapolis. You can catch a flight to Rochester from there. I could fly you to Grand Island in the Baron, but it would cost you about five hundred dollars.

Tom said, "That's out."

Looking at both of us, he said, "Are you checked out in a Lincoln Mark IV?"

I said, "Of course."

"You can take my car and drop him off at Grand Island, then bring my car back. Maybe I'll have your plane fixed tomorrow and you can pick him up in Rochester."

Before I could say no, Tom immediately said, "That would be awesome, thank you!"

I gave a tired sigh and said, "I'll take that cup of coffee now."

After turning out the lights and closing up the hangar, Jay brought the car to the front of the hangar and we climbed in. It was the kind that has those headlights that fold away when they're not being used.

Almost as an afterthought, Jay said, "Oh, there's just one little problem. The lights tend to turn off from time to time, and when they do, they fold up. But just cycle the light switch a couple of times and they'll come back on."

Tom looked at me and said, "You're driving."

It was three-thirty in the morning when we dropped off Jay in front of his house. As we said goodbye, we introduced ourselves and exchanged phone numbers.

He said, "The tank is full and there's a Nebraska state road map in the glove box. Just take this street out till you hit Highway 83, then turn right and head north. I'm sure you can use the map to find the rest of the way. Good luck."

Somehow, he made it sound like we were going to need it. We drove off into the blackness of Midwest farmland.

There were no streetlights when we got out of town, and because of the overcast and rain, there was no moon or stars – just the glow of the headlights beyond the smeared windshield wipers that were overdue to be replaced.

The Mark IV was a big, heavy car, quiet and smooth. It was one of those cars that went very fast, very easily. And we were in a hurry. Tom promptly went to sleep.

A sign said, "North Platte, 65 miles." I was doing about eighty miles per hour, and we were about fifteen minutes out of town. The road was dark and narrow, with ditches on either side.

The car, not wanting to make Jay a liar, suddenly went completely dark.

The dashboard lights went out too. It's hard to imagine how dark it got. I hit the brakes, trying to remember if the road was straight when I'd last seen it. I slowed down in as straight a line as possible, all the while frantically cycling the light switch as Jay had advised.

Feeling the braking and swerving, and hearing my swearing, Tom bolted straight up in his seat. He was now wide awake as I struggled with the speeding car in the dark.

After about six interminably long seconds, the lights came on again. To my great relief, the road was still there.

Tom said, "How am I supposed to get any sleep when you do that?"

"When *I* do that? Hey, if I can't sleep, you can't sleep."

"Well, I guess someone's gotta keep an eye on you."

"Why don't you get that map out and figure out how to get us to Grand Island?"

This kind of adrenaline shock happened five more times before the sun came up. Each time, it scared the bejeezus out of us.

We were fatigued and disoriented and started to feel like we were in some bizarre Stephen King novel in which the car was trying to kill us.

As if one emergency that night hadn't been enough.

Somewhere in the black night, we found the turnoff for Highway 23 at Maywood. We followed it until the junction of 283, then turned north toward Lexington.

The rain had stopped as we picked up Interstate 80. The eastern sky was starting to glow a pale pink.

After the first blackout, Tom had been unable to sleep, so we made small talk as he helped keep me awake.

Tom said, "I can't believe how lucky we were to find that guy in the middle of the night."

Thinking of one of my favorite authors, Richard Bach, I said, "Nothing happens by chance."

He said, "Maybe, if you believe that sort of thing. Hey, man, I apologize for getting you into this situation."

Glancing over at him in the dark car, I laughed. "No way, bro, this is an adventure. I wouldn't have it any other way. I'm enjoying this."

He said, "You really are crazy."

Now on the interstate, I kept the speed down to seventy. The national speed limit was still fifty-five. In the blue/grey misty morning light, my bleary eyes strained to look for cops. Getting a speeding ticket would only slow us down more.

We were on a mission.

I marveled at the strange fact that yesterday I'd been at work at the motorhome factory in Hemet, California, and this morning I was driving along in someone else's homicidal car, looking at signs that said, "Omaha 185 miles" and "Chicago 650 miles."

Now, as we motored smoothly on Interstate 80, it was five-thirty. Tom asked, "How far to Grand Island?"

"About an hour. Jay said he thinks the flight leaves at seven-thirty. We should get there in time."

When we pulled into the parking lot in front of the little terminal at Central Nebraska Regional Airport, the eastern sky was turning from faint pink to azure, but the sun would be a while yet.

Walking into the terminal, we were happy to find that the ticket counter was already open at six-thirty.

Tom paid for his ticket to Minneapolis and then Rochester, with no bags to check. The girl behind the counter looked at him suspiciously. He mumbled something about it being an emergency.

It turned out the flight did not leave until eight-thirty. He came back waving his ticket and said, "What do you say we get some breakfast? We haven't eaten in a while."

"Sounds good to me."

We were the only ones in the airport coffee shop besides the waitress. She wasn't very friendly; maybe it was too early for that. Or perhaps it was our longish hair and beards. This was rural America, after all, not the big city. The food came: ham and eggs for me, pancakes for Tom.

All was going well until I started pouring sugar into my coffee. The lid came off and most of the contents of the full sugar jar fell into my cup.

I numbly stared at it for a couple of seconds, then picked up the lid, screwed it back onto the jar, and placed it back in its position on the table near the salt and pepper.

It was then that I realized that Tom was laughing hysterically.

I looked out the window at the brightening sky and tried to ignore him, but it didn't work. Soon, I was laughing too. Before long, we couldn't talk or breathe. We were laughing so hard, tears were rolling down our cheeks.

The waitress frowned at us and shook her head, probably wondering what kind of drugs we were on and wishing the interstate didn't bring in such riff-raff.

There was no way she could have known what kind of night we'd had.

Chapter 16
Grand Island

*"That light at the end of the tunnel
may very well be a freight train."*

As Tom left to board his flight, I said, "Good luck with your dad. I hope he makes it."

He said, "Me too. Here's two hundred dollars, maybe enough to pay for repairs on the Bonanza. If not, it's enough to fly you home."

I thanked him and walked back out into the now bright sunlight to the Lincoln. I was happy that I didn't have to worry about its treachery on dark lonely roads anymore.

With the sun at my back, I found my way to the interstate and started cruising west on I-80, trying to remember how to get back to McCook.

I hadn't gone far when I realized that my eyelids had suddenly become the consistency of lead. They were so heavy, I was sure I wouldn't be able to keep them open any longer.

When I saw a rest stop, I pulled in and parked. Climbing into the backseat, I stretched out, marveling at how roomy it was and briefly contemplating what else you could do in such a big backseat. Soon, oblivious to the noise of passing trucks, I was sound asleep.

When I awoke two hours later, it was ten-thirty. I felt surprisingly rested and ready to go.

About noon, somewhere around Kearney, I looked in the rearview mirror to see a black and white police car that looked like it was out of the "Blues Brothers" movie. He was right on my bumper and had his red lights on.

I'd been nailed by a Nebraska State Trooper for speeding.

Being as I was from out of state, he said I had to follow him to the county seat and pay the fine in front of the justice of the peace in the little town of Elm Creek. If I didn't, he'd put me in jail.

Fortunately, Tom had given me some money. I'd seen this tactic years ago in Utah when riding through in a pack of Harleys, so I dutifully followed him into town. Appearing before a very self-important judge, I solemnly admitted guilt and paid the forty-dollar fine.

As I left the building, I imagined the two of them splitting the loot, twenty dollars each. They had just paid for their lunch and dinner.

Free again, back on the interstate, driving the homicidal Lincoln, I shook my head. I had just flown across half the country at one hundred seventy-five miles per hour only to get a ticket for driving sixty-eight in a fifty-five.

But at least it was daylight.

After I left the interstate, it seemed like endless hours of two-lane roads. I saw low rolling hills and fields of wheat and corn and other crops that I couldn't identify. They'd all been hidden in the darkness last night.

The land yacht cruised smoothly and quietly, taking up the whole lane of the narrow, old country road. Fatigue was creeping back upon me, so I used the electric button to put the window down and get some air.

It was almost three o'clock in the afternoon when I pulled back up in front of Jay's house.

After knocking on the door, I was greeted by his smiling face. "You made it," he declared, sounding surprised.

"Yeah, your car tried to make sure I didn't, but I got the upper hand."

"Come on in! You've got to be exhausted. Did Tom make the flight?"

"Yeah, with time to spare. I can't thank you enough. Would it be possible to get a ride to a motel?"

"No need for that. We've got the guest bed ready for you. Follow me."

Being from California, I was still amazed that people in small-town America were so friendly, generous, and trusting.

In a daze, I followed him down a hallway. How's it looking on the Bonanza?" I asked.

"We'll have to look at it tomorrow. I've been flying a charter flight today in the Baron. For now, you need some rest."

Jay opened the door to a small bedroom with a single bed. It was decorated for a child. There were Star Wars posters on the wall and model airplanes on a shelf.

He said, "Sleep as long as you need to. I'll see you when you get up."

"Thanks, man. I don't know how we got lucky enough to find you."

He laughed and said, with a wink, "Better lucky than good." Stepping into the hallway, he closed the door. Barely conscious, I stripped off my clothes, collapsed into the little bed, and slept a dreamless sleep. It had been a rather long day.

All too soon, Jay's wife woke me for dinner. Knocking softly on the door, she called out with a sweet Midwest accent from the other side of the door. "Time to eat. You must be hungry. Please join us."

I struggled out of the deep dark well of slumber, trying to remember where I was. What was this room? Whose house was this? What state was I in?

I dragged myself out of the bed and got dressed. Through the window, it was light blue. Dusk? Dawn? I couldn't tell. Was this breakfast or dinner?

I sat at the table in a brain fog. I don't think I was very good company. I could see that it was getting darker outside, and I remember two little kids who asked a lot of questions. I'm not sure that I had a lot of answers. It felt like I was still in a dream.

After dinner, I excused myself, then stumbled back to the little bed and crawled between the sheets. I felt as if I was entering a long, dark tunnel that got narrower and narrower.

I only knew that I felt safe in the hands of friends and, at the moment at least, no airplanes and no cars were trying to kill me.

The next morning, I opened my eyes and felt almost normal. The sun was shining through the window and I realized that I was in the middle of the great American heartland, where most of the wheat and corn are grown.

It oddly felt like home, although I'd never lived there. But it felt so normal; I couldn't shake that feeling.

Through the wispy drapes, I could see blue sky and cornfields in the distance and hear cows mooing.

It was Sunday morning. At seven o'clock, there was a knock at the door and a voice asked if I wanted to join them for breakfast.

I did.

Over a big pile of scrambled eggs and thick sliced bacon, toast, and lots of hot coffee, Jay explained that we could pull the propeller off the Bonanza and see what kind of parts he had to order.

"If you want, you can go to the hangar with me and help."

I said, "Absolutely."

It was weird, but I already felt like part of their family. It was a nice feeling for one who had never been comfortable in family atmospheres.

Later, at the airport, we went to work on the Bonanza. I helped with pulling the cowlings off and handing him tools, like a nurse handing scalpels and clamps to a surgeon.

Jay said, "Just like I figured. The propeller pitch adjustment bearing disintegrated."

"That would explain the smell of smoke and sparks in our faces the other night."

"Yeah, it's an old design. I know I can get the parts, but it may take a while, and we're not going to be able to order them today. Everything will be closed. It may take as much as a week for the parts to get here."

"I was supposed to be back to work on Monday."

"I know there are no flights out of Kansas City to L.A. on Sunday. Can you call in and tell them you'll be on your way tomorrow?"

"Yeah, that'll work."

"In the morning, I have to fly that Sierra over there to Denver to get a new gyro installed. If you want to go with me, when we get back, I'll take you over to Kansas City Airport. They have a direct flight to Los Angeles from there."

Always up for flying anywhere, I said, "Sure, that sounds great."

I spent another pleasant evening at Jay's house with his family. This time, I was rested and coherent enough to have a conversation after dinner.

I felt like I'd suddenly been adopted. Once again, I marveled at the generosity and trust of middle America.

Even though I'd experienced this before, I always found it amazing how sometimes people would open their homes to a traveling stranger.

Sitting in the living room, with the kids watching "Buck Rogers in the 25th Century," Jay and I were sipping cans of beer when he asked, "Have you ever seen Bob Hoover fly?"

"Oh, yeah, at the Mojave Air Races a few months back. He's amazing! He had Cliff Robertson riding with him in the back of his Mustang while he did the show in it, but I was really impressed with the way he flies that Shrike, shutting down the engines and all."

"Well, he's going to be here next June for my airshow."

"No way! You know Bob Hoover? You put on an airshow?"

"Sure, he comes back every year. Beechcraft helps me sponsor the airshow. There will be other famous fliers like Corkey Fornof and Bubba Beal. It's a fun time. You should plan to come out for it."

Flying halfway across the country to attend an airshow didn't sound very feasible to me on my current income.

Hesitantly, I said, "It sounds great. I'd love to come, but I'm not sure I can make it."

"Well, if you can get away to come and you don't have a way to get here, let me know. I'll arrange it so you can ride back with Bob."

My mind pulled back as I thought, 'This guy is full of crap. Me, ride with Bob Hoover? There's no way that would happen.'

But I said, "That would be awesome. I'll let you know."

The rest of the evening devolved into flying stories and talking about airplanes. Before long, we said goodnight and hit the sack.

Jay Johnson and the author, McCook, Nebraska, 1979.

Chapter 17
Jay Johnson

"A day without sunshine is like, you know, night."
~ **Steve Martin**

And they have a lot of sunshine in Nebraska.

I woke up again to the smell of breakfast and coffee – a life as natural and wholesome as the fresh-baked bread with real butter on the breakfast table.

It seemed so perfect; I had this odd feeling that maybe I was in the wrong place in California. Maybe I really belonged here.

Jay was the kind of person you felt you'd known forever. Early to mid-thirties (I never asked), he was physically fit with a youthful exuberance and a mop of blond hair hanging over his forehead. He looked more like a California surfer dude than a Midwest airplane nut who ran a Beechcraft dealership.

After breakfast, we drove to the airport and opened the hangar for the flight to Denver. We readied the Beechcraft Sierra, a low-wing four-seater with retractable landing gear and a more than adequate two hundred horsepower motor with a more modern constant-speed propeller.

It was Beechcraft's equivalent of Piper's Arrow.

When it was time to go, he said, "You want to drive?"

I'd never flown a Sierra, but said, "I'll be glad to."

Jay tossed me a VFR sectional with a circle around our destination and said, "Take the left seat. Here's where we're going. Let's hit it."

It was similar to the Bonanza, only newer. The controls were straightforward. I needed very little instruction. Off we went.

Jay was a CFII, which stands for Certificated Flight Instructor – Instrument. That meant he was qualified to teach not only flying, but also instrument flying, i.e., aviating and navigating solely by the instrument panel.

Not only did I have a temporary adopted family, but I'd been adopted by a flight instructor. He acted as my teacher on this flight for free. I already had a fair amount of experience, but I learned a few things and we had a great time flying together.

His enthusiasm for aviation was infectious – not that I needed any encouragement.

It can be amazing where life leads you. That has been a constant in my life once I got out into the world.

Because my flight into McCook had been during the dark of night, I was surprised at the view as we climbed to our cruising altitude. Western Nebraska looked as flat as a pancake. Of course, from the ground, it wasn't. Low hills, ravines, rivers, and creeks break up the landscape.

But none of that was apparent from the air. It was the same all the way to Denver. Eastern Colorado was no different from Nebraska or Kansas. Everywhere I looked were vast expanses of farmland – the breadbasket of the country, if not the world.

After one hour and forty-two minutes, at the tower controllers' instructions, flying the final approach to runway 26R as fast as we could to stay ahead of the airliners on final behind us, we landed at Denver Stapleton. They said to clear the active runway as soon as possible and we did.

Now that we were on the ground, I thought we could relax, but Jay was amused as I struggled to follow the rapid-fire instructions of the ground controllers.

It was a long taxi and we frequently had to wait for big jets – mostly from United Airlines, as this was their base – to cross in front of us. Sometimes we had to scurry out of their way as the ground controller impatiently growled and verbally frowned at us. They didn't really want us there.

I apologized to Jay: "I'm not used to this big an airport and this much radio traffic."

He chuckled and said, "You're doing fine. Don't let them rattle you. We have as much right to be here as the big boys." He seemed to be enjoying this and was quite at home in this environment.

While waiting for the gyro to be installed, it seemed like we had just eaten breakfast, so we sat in the air-conditioned lounge of the FBO, drinking their free coffee.

I was enthralled by the highly professional aviation world around us and wanted to be part of it.

With the gyro installed, we were soon on our way, sitting on a taxiway in a slow trundling line of airliners.

Jay said, "Welcome to the elephant walk."

In our Lilliputian airplane, we breathed our lungs full of jet exhaust as we made our way to the runway.

I was in the pilot's seat again. It seemed that Jay was determined to let me get as much experience on this trip as possible. I liked that arrangement.

Once we were airborne, the departure controller kept us low and out of the way of the fast-moving jets as we fled eastbound from the beehive of activity.

Back over the flat landscape and away from the constant radio chatter, the world was peaceful again. With a tailwind, the trip back was only an hour and a half.

Landing at McCook seemed a world away from the chaos of Denver. I thought about how nice it was to have this oasis of your own to fly out of.

McCook had started as a World War II training airport, a relic of America's past. However, unlike a lot of old airports, it was active and well taken care of.

It suddenly seemed like an island paradise of aviation. The only things missing were palm trees.

After I shut down the motor and the gyros did their slow winding-down song, Jay asked, "Do you have your logbook handy?"

I pulled it out of the small flight bag I carried and he filled it out for the three-hour and twelve-minute round-trip flight. He signed me off in the Sierra. "Okay to solo."

He said, "It's almost three o'clock. Your flight leaves at six-thirty. If we get going now, you'll have time to spare. We'll take the Baron. Want to fly a twin?"

I answered his smile with an even bigger one. "I can't wait!"

"I'll put the flight on Tom's bill, the Baron is a pig on gas."

I said, "I really appreciate the lift. I thought I'd have to take the bus."

He laughed.

We parked the Sierra in the hangar and pulled out the Baron. I climbed into the left seat again, as directed, throwing my jacket and flight bag into the middle seats behind us.

Jay said, "There are clouds moving into the Kansas City area. It should still be VFR when we get there, but I filed an IFR flight plan."

"I'm not IFR-qualified yet."

"That's okay. Just do what I tell you to do. It should be well above minimums for our arrival."

I had only a vague idea of what that meant, but I took his word for it. He would keep us safe.

Hesitant, I said, "I've never flown a multi-engine airplane before."

"Just operate the throttles and props together. As long as we don't lose one, we'll be fine."

"What if we do lose one?"

"Then I'll take over. See that switch? Turn it on… See those boost pumps? Turn them both on."

And so it went, with Jay telling me step by step how to start the airplane, one engine at a time. I was now operating a high-performance multi-engine airplane. It was magical, like I was in the Land of Oz, but that was Kansas, just a bit south.

As we taxied toward the runway, he said, "Easy on the brakes, those two motors will push us faster than we need, and we don't want to heat them up."

As we lined up on the runway, the Baron was powerful and responsive. Pushing the throttles up on those big engines was a thrill. When I pulled back on the yoke, it leaped into the air.

When we were airborne, Jay had me retract the landing gear. Then, at the right time, he told me to retract the flaps and how to adjust the throttles, props, and mixtures.

Soon, we were climbing to eleven thousand feet for the two-hour flight to Kansas City. As he showed me how to synchronize the propellers, I felt like a real pilot.

It had already been a long day. We chatted between radio calls from air traffic control. Behind us the sun was setting as we reached the outskirts of Kansas City.

Clouds were rolling into the area as we descended. Visibility dropped to about a mile, and the lower we got, the darker it got. We were still visual, 'VFR,' but just barely. It was good practice.

Jay was talking on the radio and busily dialing VOR radio frequencies and bearings, telling me to turn this way, turn that way, hold this heading, follow that radial, descend to this altitude, "And whatever you do, don't bust that altitude."

The instructions continued: "Pull the throttles back, slow to one-fifty, now slow to one-twenty."

He was working pretty hard. I knew that if he were flying, it would have been a lot easier on him.

As for me, I was having the time of my life.

In my peripheral vision, through the haze, I could see the lights of the city. However, I didn't take the time to look out the window. I didn't need to be sightseeing. Instead, I focused with all my being on the flight instruments, the navigation instruments, the throttles and the engine indications.

All too soon, in the gloomy dusk, we were rolling out on runway 19 at MKC, also known as Kansas City Downtown Airport – not MCI for Kansas City International, the new big one off to the northwest, outside of town.

Jay told the ground controller that he had a passenger drop at the terminal, so we were directed to a parking spot in front of a building that had the Western Airlines logo on it.

He showed me how to set the parking brake and said, "Leave the engines running. We won't be here long."

Grabbing my jacket and flight bag from the backseat, I followed him out and onto the right wing, then down onto the tarmac. He asked for my logbook and once again filled it out for the flight.

Not "Okay to solo this time." I didn't have a multi-engine rating… yet.

Jay handed back the logbook and stuck out his hand. As I shook it, he yelled over the idling motors of the Baron and the nearby jet engines, "I'll call you when the parts come in and the Bonanza is ready. See you when you come to pick it up."

"I can't thank you enough. I'll be looking forward to coming back."

I turned and strode toward the big, blocky concrete terminal, slipping into my jacket against the cold night air.

Chapter 18
More Determined Than Ever

> *"The only person you're destined to become is the person you decide to be."*
>
> ~Unknown

Tuesday morning, after very little sleep, I was back at my service manager job at the motorhome plant.

I went through the motions of the job as I marveled at the weekend I'd just gone through. Much of it had been in a brain fog of fatigue and seemed more like a dream than anything else.

One of Richard Bach's many books is called "Stranger to the Ground." He'd once had a feeling that he didn't belong on this planet. He really belonged in the air, almost as if an alien from another planet.

I was beginning to understand how he felt – like I didn't belong here. Certainly not behind a desk in a factory. I belonged in the cockpit of an airplane.

After the events of the weekend, I felt surer than ever that I needed to be a commercial pilot.

Tom returned from Minnesota. Not only did his father make it through the night, but he lived several more years before succumbing to his battle with cancer.

Doubling down on my focus, I started studying for the commercial written test even harder. Like all written tests by the FAA, it consisted of one hundred questions out of a possible one thousand questions.

I bought books with the one thousand questions and studied them, day after day.

At the same time, I had to learn commercial maneuvers and perform them for the flight tests.

But that wasn't enough; I also wanted a multi-engine rating.

And I needed an IFR rating, but that took more time, training, and money. I was impatient.

On November 9, almost a month after we'd dropped out of a rainy night sky into McCook, Nebraska, Tom and I arrived back to get his Bonanza.

Jay picked us up at Kansas City Downtown airport and flew us back in the Baron.

Having run the Bonanza's motor with the new propeller only on the ground, Jay suggested that I take it out for a test flight. He went with me.

It flew just fine. The engine was smooth and the propeller adjusted as it should. All was good. Life was back to normal. Tom had his airplane back and we were good to go.

Jay signed off my logbook again. This time, he gave me a biennial flight review. You need one every two years anyway and this one was free.

As we tossed our bags into the compartment behind the left wing, Jay smiled and said, "I topped off the gas. That's on your bill too."

Tom said, "You thought of everything. Thank you."

"Have a nice flight. Oh, and hey, don't forget about Hoover and my airshow in June. It's going to be a fun time. You don't want to miss it."

Thinking about what it cost to fly back and how much flight training I had planned, as well as what that would cost, I was non-committal. "I'll do my best to make it."

Jay said, "Remember my offer about riding with Hoover."

I was still full of doubt, but smiled and nodded anyway. He was such a nice guy. It bothered me a little that he made such outlandish promises.

Soon, Tom and I were climbing out of McCook Regional Airport, but not westbound. We took up a heading of one hundred fifty degrees south-south-east.

We landed in Norman, Oklahoma. It was Friday evening and we were there to party with our brothers from the motorcycle club for the weekend.

I had to be back to work on Monday, so on Sunday morning, November 11, only slightly hungover, we had breakfast with some of the boys at the airport café. This time, we were bringing along a passenger. The three of us climbed into the Bonanza and launched westbound into a clear blue sky.

Before long, we encountered clouds at lower altitudes. The headwind was brutal, about twenty-five knots, so we were going slower than normal.

We flew over the cloud layer, which was risky, though not the flying itself; it's very pleasant having the clean, white layer of clouds below you, as long as you can navigate.

We were following VOR radials westbound. Getting lost wasn't a problem. If I were in my little Cessna 140, that would have been a different story.

The risk came if something went wrong, say, an engine failure. Now you'd be forced to descend through the clouds. Assuming you could do that successfully, without losing control or picking up severe icing, when you came out the bottom of the clouds, you'd have to find a place to land.

How high the cloud layer was above the ground would determine how much time you had. And the last thing you'd want was to have to do that in the dark.

Fortunately, it wasn't dark, and when we got to the Albuquerque area, the cloud layer was gone.

After four hours and forty-two minutes, we landed at Alameda Airport, on the outskirts of Albuquerque, New Mexico.

Just across the Rio Grande River and north and west from the hustle and bustle of Albuquerque International, Alameda was a nice, quiet place to get gas. Today, sadly, it's gone – just houses and businesses.

The elevation was about four thousand feet. The day was cold.

We found some snacks and sodas in vending machines, filled up the wing tanks, and were soon on our way.

Barry, one of the Oklahoma brothers, was hitching a ride to SoCal with us, so we were fairly heavy with three grown men and full tanks.

I was the experienced pilot onboard, and my license was what made us legal. I should have thought about density altitude, factoring in our weight vs. altitude vs. temperature.

However, the cool weather lulled me, and it was turning into a long day. I needed to get home to work in the morning. It's called "get-home-I'tis."

Tom was flying as we took off to the west, the Bonanza lifted off normally. But instead of doing its normal eager climb into the sky, the airplane was very sluggish. At full power, it didn't want to accelerate, nor would it climb.

Once past the pavement of the runway, we were about thirty feet off the sagebrush. Right then, we didn't like being "Riders of the Purple Sage."

Pulling up the landing gear and flaps seemed to make no difference. Luckily, there were no big buildings, trees, or power lines ahead of us.

Tom said, "Why won't it climb or accelerate? Is there something wrong with the engine?"

I said, "No, it's the density altitude. We're too heavy for this condition."

"What should I do?"

"Just keep it straight ahead with the wings level. Try to increase your airspeed. We'll get lighter as we burn gas… as long as we don't hit anything first."

Tom snapped a glance at me and said, "That's not very encouraging."

I said, "Just focus on your airspeed and your altitude."

The sun was already down and the ground was painted in deep shadows where the canyons and ravines were located.

Still about thirty feet off the ground, the Bonanza struggled, unable to climb or gain speed. I tried to stay calm, but I was starting to sweat. Glancing toward the backseat, I saw that Barry looked pale and had a grim set to his jaw. Our eyes met for a moment, but he said nothing.

As we came upon a large canyon, the ground dropped away under us. Though it was dark in there, I told Tom, "Put the nose down and fly into that canyon. Pick up some airspeed and turn south, then follow the canyon downhill and try to get to a normal climb speed."

It worked. The ground started to fall away as the wings achieved a better lift-over-drag speed. We accelerated until the airplane climbed normally.

We'd made it. We were still alive and the airplane was in one piece! Who could ask for more?

Other than the headwinds, we had good weather the rest of the way.

Five hours later, we touched down at Hemet Airport in California.

Barry, who had been silent since the tense takeoff in Albuquerque, climbed down off the wing, stretched, yawned, and said, "The hell with you guys. Next time I'm riding my motorcycle."

I continued studying and training on my own, and with Curt's help. On March 13, 1980, I took my commercial-multi-engine check ride and passed. Another milestone.

I thought I'd go out and immediately get a flying job. Apparently, my boss at the motorhome plant thought I'd do that too. He laid me off.

The economy was in a malaise, with high unemployment, high inflation, high interest rates, and high gas prices. Hardly anyone was buying motorhomes. Sales were as low as Jimmy Carter's polling numbers. The company was losing money and they needed to get rid of people.

As much as I wanted to, I wasn't yet ready to get a flying job. A commercial pilot's license wasn't the magic you might think it was for getting hired.

Instead of looking for another job, I applied for unemployment and doubled down on my efforts to get more qualified. I spent my days studying for written exams and my nights doing flight training with Curt.

By May 29, I had taken the check ride for my IFR rating and was now fully qualified to work as a pilot.

I might not have done my flight training cheaper than anyone ever, but I think I was close. Most people pay tens of thousands of dollars for the training I had done. I didn't keep track of the money, but it was probably in the hundreds, and certainly not thousands.

Soon after my latest check ride, the phone rang. It was Jay Johnson.

"Hey, Dale, the airshow is next week. Are you coming?"

"Damn, I'd love to, Jay, but I'm not working right now and there's no way I can afford to fly back there."

"If you can get away, I'll call Bob and see if you can ride with him."

Once again, I had my doubts. Almost to call his bluff, I said, "If you can do that, I'll be there."

"I'll call you back."

An hour later, the phone rang again. Jay said, "You're all set. Take down this number. It's Jim Driskell, Bob's airshow announcer and partner. He's expecting you. I'll see you next week."

Thinking, 'This can't be real,' I thanked him, hung up, and dialed the number.

I heard Jim's cheerful voice on the other end of the line. When I told him who I was, he said, "Jay told me all about you. We'd love to have you come along. Meet me at Air Research at Los Angeles Airport at nine o'clock Thursday morning."

"How long can I hang out with you?"

"As long as you can pay your way, you can stay as long as you like."

Still not quite sure this was happening, I said, "I'll see you Thursday then."

Chapter 19
The Pilot's Pilot

"It's not too good to be true, it's so good it must be true."
~Unknown

Bob Hoover was the world's best pilot! Fighter pilot, war hero, military test pilot, civilian test pilot, airshow performer, and all-around aviation legend.

Even Chuck Yeager looked up to him; they'd been buddies for years. Bob was his backup pilot for the Bell X-1 program and was flying the chase plane next to him on the day Yeager first broke the speed of sound.

He also saved Yeager's life one day when, on a test flight, the cockpit of the X-1 iced up and there was no forward visibility. Flying alongside him in an F-80 fighter, Bob talked him down to a blind landing at Edwards Air Force Base.

General Jimmy Doolittle called Bob "the greatest stick and rudder man who ever lived." He was one of the ten most famous pilots ever, right up there with the Wright Brothers and Charles Lindbergh.

He also counted Charles Lindbergh and Neil Armstrong among his personal friends.

June 1980. I recruited my mother to drive me to LAX – a two-hour drive if you're lucky, depending on traffic. We pulled through the gate at Air Research at promptly nine o'clock.

After parking the car in front of a huge hangar, we walked into the office to find Jim Driskell doing flight planning for the trip to McCook.

With his cheery good nature, he greeted us as if we were old friends. "Great to meet you, glad you could make it. Just throw your bag in the Shrike and I'll be right out. Make sure you hit the bathroom before we go. We won't stop for gas until Denver."

Looking around, I asked, "Where's Bob?"

"Oh, he doesn't keep the Mustang here. He's flying it out of Torrance. We'll meet him in McCook. That's the way we work. He flies Old Yeller and I bring the Shrike."

I thanked my mom for the ride, gave her some money for gas, and told her, "I'll see ya when I see ya."

As I tossed my bag into Bob Hoover's Aero Commander N500RA, it didn't seem real. I'd watched him fly this airplane at the Mojave Air Races while crowds of tens of thousands watched, in awe at his skill and the maneuvers he performed. Now I was about to fly in it.

I stood alongside the Shrike in the thick gray morning air as the marine layer thinned and the sun tried to break through. Seeing the other airplanes parked or taxiing around, mostly jets, had a dreamlike quality. My current situation was even more surreal.

You just never know where life will take you.

I tried not to judge or assume. Just live in the moment with gratitude. And, boy, did I have a lot of gratitude.

I was grateful for Jay Johnson arranging this, despite my doubts. I was even grateful for the frightening night when the prop bearing had failed and the marathon night in the homicidal Lincoln, trying to get Tom to Rochester, Minnesota.

Sometimes life is like a roller coaster. All you have to do is climb in and hang on.

As Jim fired up the two-hundred-and-ninety horsepower Lycomings, I was mesmerized.

I don't want to say that I was starstruck, but… I was starstruck. This was probably one of the most famous aircraft in civil aviation since the Spirit of Saint Louis.

It was a normal business airplane, not certified for aerobatics. But, of course, Bob had a waiver from the FAA. He could make airplanes do things nobody else could do.

Taxing out onto the active taxiway, we joined a line of airliners waiting to take off.

As we slowly moved along, we breathed jet exhaust and talked about the flight for the day ahead.

I wore a headset so that I could hear the ground controller's transmissions. Our conversation always ceased when ATC talked, which was almost constantly.

Finally, it was our turn to take off on runway 25L. Compared to the big airliners, we were off the ground in no time.

Jim flew, climbing above the marine layer and into bright blue skies. We began a slow wide left turn toward the east. Looking down through the fog, I could see endless houses and streets in neighborhoods. That second engine was comforting.

Once we were heading eastbound, over Riverside and entering the desert as we climbed past Mount San Jacinto, the non-stop radio chatter died down and we could talk normally.

Jim said, "So, do you work as a pilot?"

"No, not yet, but I have my multi-engine, commercial, and just got my IFR rating last week."

Jim said, "That's great, congratulations. Have you seen Bob fly?"

"Yes, of course, at Mojave. He's incredible."

"Yes, he is. How do you know Jay?"

"Me and a buddy dropped into his airport in the middle of the night last year. He took care of us, took care of our airplane, and invited me to this airshow. So here I am."

"Jay's a hell of a guy. I'm glad this worked out. He says you're a good guy, so that's good enough for us."

Once again, I wondered… I hardly knew Jay, but he seemed to have put a lot of trust in me, to the point of recommending me to the world's best airshow performer, a legend in aviation.

How could I ever measure up to that?

As we climbed through eight thousand feet, Jim asked, "Would you like to fly it?"

Surprised, I said, "Heck yeah!" Then I hesitated. "Bob won't mind?"

"Of course not."

With a grin, I slid my seat forward, then put my hands on the control yoke and my feet on the rudder pedals.

"Okay, you've got it."

"I've got the airplane," I confirmed. The right side of the cockpit had a full set of flight and navigation instruments. I didn't have to look "cross cockpit."

"Just follow the radials that we're assigned to. We're on an IFR flight plan, so don't get off course. We'll be leveling off at eleven thousand."

Not only was I getting to fly a high-performance business twin, but I was also now flying Bob Hoover's airplane. "Happy", wasn't the word for it; I was ecstatic!

We climbed into a tailwind and streaked along in the clear air.

After twenty minutes, Jim said, "Let me know when you want the autopilot."

"Okay, I'll let you know."

I never did ask for the autopilot even though Jim would look at me sideways from time to time, then shake his head and smile. I wasn't about to waste a single minute of getting to fly this famous airplane.

Jim was a little shorter than me and a little rounder. About fifty-five years old, he seemed happy and good-natured, living a life he loved: traveling around the country, bringing the Shrike to the airshows, and narrating while Bob flew. They were a team.

I was already familiar with his enthusiastic airshow descriptions of Bob's maneuvers over the loudspeakers. To me, he was just as famous as the pilot he narrated for.

Cruising at a little under two hundred miles per hour, and with a tailwind of thirty to forty miles per hour, we made good time. I think he was happy for the company.

Three and a half hours later, we were on final to Denver Stapleton Airport to get gas. Using the throttle and propeller settings he told me to use, I slowed the airplane to approach speed.

When we put down the landing gear, Jim took back the controls, went to full flaps, and squeaked the wheels onto the runway. Then we followed the rapid-fire instructions to the FBO to get gas.

First leg down.

Though it held one hundred fifty-six gallons, Jim was careful to figure the fuel so that the airplane wouldn't have too much onboard for Bob's performance.

After a quick pit stop in the FBO, we were back in the air for the hour-and-twenty-minute flight to McCook.

Landing just before six o'clock, we saw the yellow P-51 Mustang sitting in front of the big hangar. We taxied to it and parked alongside.

Some local mechanics had the engine cowls off and were doing last-minute tweaking on a small oil leak.

It turned out that Bob had already left for the hotel with Jay, so the mechanics directed us to the rental car that had been supplied for us.

When we arrived at the hotel, a room was waiting with my name on it. I paid cash and dropped off my bag before joining Jim in the bar for drinks and dinner.

When I walked in, it was a party atmosphere. There was a crowd near the bar and in the center was Bob Hoover, holding court with a drink in one hand and telling flying stories as his audience listened intently.

Jim was already there and waved me over. As I squeezed through the small crowd, Bob had just finished a story that was greeted by raucous laughter.

Jim grabbed my arm and pulled me into the center of the gathering. He announced to Bob and everybody present, "This is the guy I was telling you about. He's going to be traveling with us for a while and helping us out with the airshows."

Bob immediately stuck out his hand and said, in his smooth Tennessee accent, "I'm very pleased to meet you. Thanks for coming along with us."

I was barely able to mumble, "My pleasure, thanks for having me."

I realized: He was thanking me? He was a perfect gentleman every time I was around him, to me and to anyone else he dealt with.

I hadn't even noticed Jay Johnson standing next to him until he spoke up and said, with a big grin, "Welcome back. Thanks for coming."

Shaking his hand, I said, "Good to see you again. Thank you for setting this up. I still can't believe it."

The group of Bob's admirers looked at me a bit enviously for being part of this inner circle. They probably wondered, "Who the heck is this guy?"

Someone spoke up and said, "Hey, Bob, tell us about the time you stole the Messerschmitt fighter in Germany."

"It wasn't a Messerschmitt, it was a Focke-Wulf One-Ninety, and…"

As he launched into the story, he first had to explain how he had escaped from the prisoner-of-war camp. Not wanting to waste time looking at a menu, I ordered a cheeseburger and a beer and listened just as raptly as everybody else.

I'd had a long and exciting day, having left Hemet, California early that morning and then hand flying most of the flight from Los Angeles to McCook.

I tried to memorize every word as Bob told story after story. He kept the group laughing almost constantly with his sense of humor.

He wasn't so much rattling off stories as he was answering questions people asked, but each time the answer seemed to turn into a great story. At fifty-eight, Bob had lived a life that was more interesting than any novel.

Even my new friend, Jim Driskell, listened and laughed, though I'm sure he'd heard those stories a thousand times.

Finally, the crowd started to thin out. Jim turned to me and said, "I'll pick you up in front of your room at seven o'clock sharp."

With that, he and Bob excused themselves, saying that they would see everyone at the airport in the morning. I finished my burger and a second beer, then headed to my room in a daze. It was like I was living in a dream.

Chapter 20
Like Joining the Circus

*"The biggest adventure you can take is to **live** the life of your dreams."*
~Oprah Winfrey

Jim was right on time, seven o'clock. He handed me a paper cup with coffee as I climbed into the rental car. Off we went to the airport.

Bob was already there, talking to the mechanics who were still working on that oil leak. He saw us and came over to the car as we climbed out.

"That oil leak isn't a big deal. I can still fly the shows even if they don't get it fixed."

Jim asked, "How does the gas in the Shrike look? We had pretty good tailwinds coming in here from Denver."

"It's about a hundred pounds more than I'd like." Glancing at me with a sly smile, Bob said to Jim, "Why don't you take Dale up for a spin and burn off about eighteen or twenty gallons?"

I think my mouth dropped open, but Jim looked at me with that grin of his and said, "How 'bout an official checkout in the Shrike?"

All I could do was nod and smile.

Like a good flight instructor, Jim put me in the left seat: Bob Hoover's seat! He showed me how to start the engines. I was already used to where the engine and flight instruments were.

After the starter engaged, each motor roared to life. Because this was a business airplane, the cabin was well insulated, and we could still talk in normal voices without the busy radio chatter of the big airports of the day before.

Jim talked on the radio as he instructed me as to which taxiway to take to the active runway.

Advancing those throttles to takeoff power and feeling the acceleration was magical. The Shrike lifted off easily. I retracted the landing gear, then the flaps when Jim told me to.

When we leveled at five thousand feet, Jim pulled back one engine, simulating a failure. Having just completed multi-engine training a few months before, I knew what to do for single-engine flight. He told me what airspeed to maintain, and I did shallow turns in both directions.

As soon as that was done, he fed the dead engine back to life. Once I got the trim knobs secured, he pulled off the other engine.

It was great practice. I couldn't help but be amazed, this was what Bob would do with this airplane during his performances – only then he'd be doing rolls and loops at the same time.

After restoring both engines, Jim had me do some steep turns at forty-five degrees while holding altitude. Then, all too soon, it was time to go back to the airport. The required fuel had been burned off.

On the landing, there was plenty of runway, so I held it off as long as I could and the landing was very smooth.

Jim pretended to be upset because I'd gotten such a good touchdown, but I could tell he was impressed.

As we rolled out on the runway, a pheasant flashed in front of us and flew into the propeller. Jim shook his head and said, "Well, I'll be… I've killed plenty of pheasants with a shotgun, but never with an airplane."

As we shut down the engines, he asked where my logbook was. Pulling it out of my flight bag, we sat in the quiet cockpit as Jim entered the half an hour of flight time and signed it with his CFII credentials.

When we told Jay about the pheasant, he jumped in his car and drove out to get it off the runway. When he brought it back, he said, "The propeller took the head clean off. I'm going to take it home and we'll have it for dinner. No point in letting him go to waste."

Jim laughed and said, "Maybe we should paint a pheasant on the side of the cockpit for the kill."

It was Friday and the airshows weren't until Saturday and Sunday. Bob was busy taking the Mustang up to test out the oil leak. Because the mechanics wouldn't take money to work on his plane, he was giving them rides in the backseat.

The P-51 was a single-seat airplane, but behind the pilot was a space that had originally been filled with radio racks and electronics. Modern solid-state radios are very small and light, so there was plenty of room behind the pilot once those big old racks were taken out.

Now, bolted to the floor, was the plastic or fiberglass seat from a patio chair. When I saw Bob Hoover fly at the Mojave Air Races, he had actor Cliff Robertson, a pilot himself, sitting in that seat during his airshows in the Mustang.

Friday was an easy day. Bob, while checking out his oil leak, practiced his routine in the Mustang, with happy – and sometimes airsick – mechanics riding in the little bucket seat behind him.

It wasn't such an easy day for Jay Johnson, our host. He was very busy running back and forth and talking on a radio, trying to make everything run smoothly for the weekend's airshow.

Soon, we found ourselves back in the bar at the hotel. Bob and Jim drank mixed drinks, while I had beer. Another group of fans crowded around Bob, asking him questions and eliciting more legendary stories.

He seemed very comfortable in that environment, hanging out with his admirers. When he wasn't flying, he loved talking about flying.

I was around him a lot, but so was everyone else. It seemed there was always a crowd, so I got to talk with him very little – just brief conversations.

The bar shut down at midnight, so we did too. I was having the time of my life.

I was back at the airport in the morning. The next two days were a blur. Between running errands for Bob or Jim, I was meeting famous fliers like Corkey Fornof, Kermit Weeks, and Bubba Beal. Of course, all of them knew and were friends with Bob and Jim.

Corkey Fornof flew in with his BD-5J, the world's smallest jet. It was the same one he later flew through a hangar in the James Bond movie "Octopussy." Corkey went on to become a famous stunt pilot and aerial coordinator for hundreds of Hollywood movies and television shows. He did an aerobatic routine in the tiny jet both Saturday and Sunday.

The author with Corkey Fornof at McCook, Nebraska.

Before the flying started, I was sent in the rental car to another of the hotels in town to pick up Kermit Weeks. He was already a two-time winner of the National Champion Aerobatic competition and, over a period of a dozen years, placed in the top three in the world five times at the World Aerobatic Championships.

He performed in the airshow both days in his "Weeks Special," wowing the crowd with his maneuvers.

Also present was Harold "Bubba" Beal in his Grumman F8F Bearcat. Watching it fly and listening to that huge Pratt & Whitney R-2800 engine, producing as much as twenty-eight hundred horsepower in emergency mode, was a delight.

It turned out that Jim's eyesight wasn't what it used to be, and he had trouble keeping Bob's airplane in sight during the aerobatic exhibition.

When Bob was out climbing back up for more altitude and making his turns back to the airport, Jim kept shutting off the microphone and asking me, "Where is he? What's he doing now?"

Bubba Beal in his Grumman Bearcat. Photo by the author.

So, I became part of the routine, serving as Jim's eyes and calling out Bob's location and direction so that Jim would be ready to explain what maneuver Bob would be presenting to the crowd next.

The top billing for any airshow was Bob Hoover – unless the Thunderbirds or the Blue Angels were there. And when they were, they would stand in line just to meet him, shake his hand, and get their picture taken with him.

He would do two shows a day, one in each airplane, just as I had seen him do at the air races in the desert of Mojave Airport.

Everyone loved to watch the Mustang and hear its powerful Rolls-Royce Merlin engine screaming by. He would do loops and rolls – all typical airshow fare.

The show I really loved was when he'd roll the Shrike upside down on take-off before the gear was even up. Then he'd shut down one engine and roll into it. When you're learning to fly multi-engine airplanes, they tell you to not even turn into the dead engine.

He'd do a whole series of acrobatic maneuvers with one engine shut down and the propeller feathered. And as if that wasn't enough, he'd then shut down both engines and do the same thing.

His finale was to dive toward the runway with both engines shut down and the props feathered. Both engines were obviously off.

It was always eerie to listen to the whistling of the wings and fuselage cutting through the air as he leveled off just feet from the runway at two hundred eighty miles per hour, with no engine noise. It sounded like a jet, only not as loud.

From there, he'd pull straight up into a loop, then back down within feet of the runway, nose up again, and do an eight-point roll.

Turning away from the runway, he'd widen out for a two-hundred-seventy-degree turn back to the runway as he put down the landing gear.

Sometimes, if he had enough airspeed and altitude, he would do another barrel roll with the gear down as he turned his final approach to the runway.

He'd do what he called his "Tennessee Waltz," side slipping the airplane back and forth in his descent, then touch down on one main wheel, pick the airplane back up, and then touch down on the other main wheel.

Finally, he'd set it down on the runway, pick a taxiway, and roll to a stop in the same spot next to the Mustang from where he'd left.

Bob passing in front of the crowd with both engines shut down.
Photo by the author.

All of this last maneuver was done with the engines off before he dived from altitude.

After he parked, he'd climb out, take off his Panama hat, and wave as his fans cheered. Then he'd walk to the crowd, shake hands, and sign autographs.

He was called "The Pilots' Pilot." I've never seen anyone replicate this kind of flying skill.

At this time, in 1980, he wore a business suit and tie. Some years later, after having the Mustang catch fire at an airshow, he was able to land it and escape unharmed. After that, he wore a fireproof Nomex flight suit.

The weekend was a blur of activity. Immediately after the show on Sunday, Bob was always the last to perform. It was a little after two o'clock when Jim and I threw our bags into the Shrike and left the rental car with Jay Johnson.

The crowd started thinning out as we filed a flight plan while the Shrike was being refueled. Immediately after, we took off and headed west into the afternoon sun. Jim took the left seat, but he let me fly from the right, which I was happy to do.

One hour and twenty-four minutes later, we touched down at Tri-County Airport just east of Boulder, Colorado and a little north and west of Denver's Stapleton Airport.

It was late afternoon, but we had gained an hour in the Mountain Time Zone. Bob was already there, having smoked past us overhead in that speedy Mustang.

Again, parking next to it, we climbed out and found Bob talking with the owner of the small private airport. They were discussing the details of the afternoon's airshow.

Unlike the previous two days, with numerous flyers, Bob was to be the sole attraction for this short Sunday evening performance.

The parking ramps were closed off with barriers and a crowd was beginning to form on the other side.

I don't remember the name of the proprietor of this airport, but he was putting on quite a party. A live band, The Kingston Trio, would be performing on a stage that was actually a flatbed truck.

The group had been big in the sixties. By 1980, they were maybe not quite as popular, but I liked their music and I thought it was great to get to see them live.

There was free food and drink, with an open bar – and an airshow with the famous Bob Hoover. It was a great way to spend a Sunday afternoon.

When it was time for Bob's demonstration, he started with the Mustang as usual. The crowd loved watching that beautiful, powerful beast of a fighter plane as he wrung it out. I resumed my now familiar role of being Jim's eyes as Bob drifted out of sight while climbing to altitude and turning back to the airport.

Next was the Shrike, with the usual engine shutdowns, aerobatics, and a dead stick landing, all to the sheer joy of the crowd as they responded with cheers and applauds.

But this time, there was a finale, something I didn't expect. Someone at the airport owned a Fly Baby. Picture a tiny, open-cockpit, fabric-covered airplane that would have been a biplane if it had a top wing. It didn't, it was a low-wing open cockpit airplane.

The owner offered it to Bob to fly if he wanted to. Of course, Bob not only wanted to fly it, but he also proceeded to put on his regular performance in it.

It was just like in the Mustang: rolls, loops, eight-point rolls, sixteen-point rolls, landing on one main wheel, then the other, of course the crowd loved it.

The little airplane – which Bob, at six-foot-two, barely fit into – was so slow that the whole routine was performed right in front of the crowd, without the long turnarounds of the faster planes. I didn't have to spot for Jim this time.

When the aerial demonstrations were over, it was almost dark. That amounted to five airshow performances Bob had done that day, not including the high-speed hop from McCook to Tri-County Airport.

I marveled at his stamina and dedication. At that time, he was fifty-eight years old. You have to love flying, doing those routines were hard work.

The crowd now moved to the makeshift flatbed trailer stage to watch The Kingston Trio perform. It was a great show. I recognized all the songs they played from hearing them on the radio years earlier. They were a big hit with the audience.

There was a buffet of barbecued ribs, coleslaw, salad, fresh corn on the cob, and biscuits, all you could eat. I helped myself, as food had been rather scarce during the work of the last two days.

The open bar was nice, as I didn't have to pay for a beer, but after just two, Jim and Bob grabbed me and we piled into a rental car. The three of us headed for the hotel they had reserved. We had travel plans. In the morning, we were going to the big airshow in Reading, Pennsylvania.

Chapter 21
Mistakes

"Mistakes are part of the dues one pays for a full life."
~ **Sophia Loren**

At seven o'clock Monday morning, Jim was knocking on my door again. Already dressed, I opened it. Jim pushed a cup of coffee from the office into my hand and said, "Bob already took a cab to the airport. We'll meet him there. We got a phone call. The power is out, and we won't be able to get gas."

As we walked into the small operations room of the airport, Bob turned to us and said, "The driver of the semi-truck for The Kingston Trio's stage got a little too friendly with the open bar last night.

"About two o'clock, he was leaving with that long flatbed trailer and cut the corner onto the road out front. He took out the telephone pole and all of the power within several blocks, including the airport."

Jim said, "How long before they restore the power?"

"Don't know. They say the utility company is on the way. I've got enough gas in the Mustang to hop over to Stapleton. I can fill up there and head to Reading."

Jim asked, "How's the fuel in the Shrike?"

"Too low after the show last night. You should wait 'till they get the power on and fill it up here."

Cheerily, Jim said, "Okay, we'll be in Reading as soon as we can."

As Jim walked away, Bob turned to me and said, "I'd really like to take you with me to Reading, but I've got only one parachute… If that bird catches on fire at altitude, there's no way we could get it down in time. We'd have to bail out, and…"

He was actually apologizing for not being able to let me ride with him in the Mustang.

I picked up the cue and said, "Hey, no problem. I'd love to ride with you, but I understand. There'll be another chance."

He smiled, put his hand on my shoulder, and said, "I'll see you in Reading."

I had seen the mechanics in McCook riding with him and was envious, hoping I might get a chance to do that – while at the same time worrying that if I did, and got airsick, I would be mortified.

But their airshow schedule was going to last about six weeks and I'd been with them for only five days. I'd do anything to stay with them as long as possible, and I was sure there would be another opportunity.

Standing in the operations room, we heard the beautiful music of the Mustang's big Merlin engine fire up. A young man who had been standing behind the counter walked up to Jim and said, "I'm the line boy here. If you need gas, we have a hand pump. I can pump you some gas. What'll you need?"

Jim said, "Twenty-five gallons should be more than enough to get us to Denver."

It was over fifteen hundred miles to Reading, Pennsylvania. At an average of one hundred and eighty miles per hour, depending on tailwinds, we were looking at eight and a half hours minimum.

Being anxious to get in the air, Jim said, "That sounds good to me. Let's do it."

I waited in the operations room while Jim followed him out, got in, and fired up the Shrike, taxing it to where the hand pump was located.

In Alaska and many remote locations, vehicles and airplanes are routinely fueled by hand from fifty-five-gallon drums. When the line boy said, "hand pump," that was what I pictured.

While the manual fueling operation was in progress, Jim came back in and filed an IFR flight plan to Omaha, where we would make our first gas stop on our way to Reading. We could pick up the flight plan after topping off in Denver in thirty minutes.

As we walked back to the Shrike, the line boy was pulling the ladder away from the wing. He said, "You're all set, twenty-five gallons."

Jim said, "What do I owe you?"

The guy said, "Don't worry about it, we're glad to help out. Sorry about the inconvenience."

He had no idea.

Thanking him, we climbed into the Shrike and threw our bags in the backseat. Jim had a front door on the left side. I climbed through the large passenger door on the left side and walked in a crouch to the cockpit to strap into the right seat.

Jim hit the starter on the left engine, and it roared to life. Immediately, he started the right engine. It did the same. He released the parking brake and we started to move.

We rolled about ten feet when both engines quit.

Jim said, "What the hell?"

With no hesitation, he hit the left engine starter again. It fired briefly, then sputtered and died.

The same thing happened with the right engine. Then neither engine would start.

He said, "I don't believe this!"

I said, "It sounds like bad gas."

"Nonsense, it can't be!"

After several more attempts to start the engines, they refused to spark or turn over.

I repeated, "I think it's water in the gas."

"It can't be."

Finally, worried about overheating the starter motors, Jim gave up. He shut down the power switches and we got out.

I asked, "Do you have a fuel sampler?"

Jim said, "Yeah, of course, just inside the back door."

He located it. When he put it under the wing to drain the fuel, it came out the consistency of Italian salad dressing – thick and oily, only those black flakes floating in the glass tube weren't pepper and spices. They were dirt. The rest was water. No wonder the engines wouldn't start.

Walking back into the operations room, Jim said to the line boy, "The motors won't start. We have a problem here."

Moisture tends to condensate inside an underground fuel tank; any fuel tank, really. Water is heavier than gas, so it sinks to the bottom of the tank.

The "sump pump" that the line boy used was designed to pump the water out of the bottom of the tank. He didn't know that. Neither did we.

He had just pumped twenty-five gallons of dirty water into the Shrike's tanks.

Jim shook his head and said, in a huge understatement, "This is not good."

The FBO that gave us the gas towed the Shrike into their hangar and started draining the wing tanks to remove the dirty water.

After about an hour, they declared it empty. By now, the power was back on, so they towed it to the gas pumps and filled it with clean gas.

A sample of some gas from the sump drain under the wing still showed dirt and water. After the process was repeated over and over, the gas came out clear.

This time, the engines started right up. Jim looked at me and said, rather grimly, "I need to test-fly it to see what happens. You stay here."

I was disappointed, but I understood. Jim, whether he liked it or not, had just become a test pilot. He didn't want any more distractions or liabilities than necessary.

I held my breath as I watched him roll down the runway and lift off. Neither engine quit; they sounded healthy and strong as he climbed away.

Ten minutes later, he was back. After he landed, as he was rolling out on the narrow runway of the small private airport, the left brake seized and locked the wheel.

I watched as blue smoke poured off the tire and the airplane skidded to the left side of the runway, flattening one of the runway lights.

I trotted across the grass as Jim shut down the engines and climbed out of the cockpit.

As I got within hearing distance, he said, "Well, don't that beat all! The other day a pheasant, now a runway light!"

We laughed to ease the tension, then pulled out the fuel sampler. It was just as cloudy and dirty as the first time.

The brake failure had nothing to do with the dirty gas, but now we had another problem to fix. Bob needed this airplane in Reading to do his regular shows and we were eight hours away.

The runway was shut down while the FBO sent out a tug and some mechanics to release the brake and bring the Shrike back into the hangar.

This wasn't the first time a line boy had accidentally sabotaged Bob's airplane.

Two years prior, at Brown Field, east of San Diego and just north of the Mexican border, a line boy had mistakenly fueled his Shrike, at that time registration number N2300H, with jet fuel.

It was after his performance on Saturday, and he was heading home to Palomar airport for the night. There would be another show the next day. Two passengers were hitching a ride. Bob, always generous and accommodating, had said, "C'mon along."

After the engines quit, Bob was able to make a successful crash landing in a canyon not far from the runway. It's possible that if the pilot had been anyone else, nobody would have survived.

This was one of the stories I heard Bob tell in a bar one night. What he didn't tell was what happened to the line boy.

I asked Jim about it later. He told me that when Bob and his passengers were brought back to Brown Field by a helicopter, which picked them up from the crash site, he went looking for the line boy.

Asking around, nobody wanted to tell him where the boy was. They were afraid that Bob was going to chew him out big time.

When he finally found him, the line boy was outside, alone, standing by a fence and crying.

Instead of chewing him out, Bob put his arm around his shoulder and said, "No one alive has ever not made a mistake and I know you'll never make that mistake again. Tomorrow, when I fly the P-51, I want you, and only you, to fuel it."

The next year, Bob bought N500RA to continue doing his full airshow routine.

At Tri-County Airport in Colorado, the Shrike was now back in the hangar, getting the brake fixed and the tanks drained again.

Twice more that day we repeated the process of checking new fuel in the tanks until it came out clean, then Jim taking it up for a test flight.

While not doing aerobatics like Bob would, he shook it around and banked the wings steeply as much as he dared. Upon landing, we would find the same dirty water in the fuel. Still, the engines never so much as sputtered.

Late in the day, Jim was able to get ahold of Bob, who was already in Reading.

After the situation was explained, they decided that we would leave in the morning and head for Pennsylvania. The conversation went something like this.

Bob said, "Jim, I need that airplane here for the airshow. How do you feel about only flying during the day, but no IFR in or above clouds and no night flying? If you had to make an emergency landing, it needs to be during daylight."

Talking on the FBO's phone at the counter, Jim said, "I'm good with that." He looked at me, and I flashed him a thumbs-up. He nodded and said, "Dale is too. We'll leave in the morning."

Jim and I headed back to the hotel for one more night.

Chapter 22
Flying on Pins and Needles

"I'm not afraid of death;
I just don't want to be there when it happens."

~ **Woody Allen**

June 10 was a Tuesday. Once again at the airport bright and early, we were lucky to have VFR weather, as we couldn't go if it wasn't.

We hadn't taken time for breakfast, so we took advantage of their free coffee and donuts, also known as pilot food.

They topped off the tanks and we nervously checked the fuel sumps from the wings to see how clean it was.

After doing this several times before the samples came out clean, we crossed our fingers, knowing by now that it wasn't going to stay that way. We climbed into the cockpit.

The takeoff and climb out were uneventful. Half an hour later, we cruised across the flat expanse of eastern Colorado in the clear sunshine, listening carefully to the engines.

We kept a nervous eye on the engine instruments, but the motors sounded healthy and never missed, belying the quality of the gas that was feeding them.

We could have gone farther, but we were both anxious to check that fuel again. The engines were running so well, we must have gotten all of the dirty water out.

Dropping back into McCook, Nebraska, we got to see Jay Johnson briefly as we took on some more gas.

Jay was surprised to see us. Jim explained what had happened at the little airport in Colorado and how we were limping the Shrike to Pennsylvania for the Reading Airshow.

Before we topped it off, we checked the sumps. Sure enough, the gas was just as dirty as it had been before.

Jim stared at the fuel sample in disbelief and said, "I don't know how this thing keeps on running."

Jay said, "I wouldn't fly an airplane like that."

"Bob needs the airplane, so we'll do what we need to do."

Jay said, "I don't envy you having to fly all the way back east in this condition. You're not going to fly at night, are you?"

Shaking his head, Jim said, "No, and not IFR either. We probably won't make it there today."

"Looks like you better get going then."

With the fueling done, we checked the sumps one more time and were still disappointed to see the same mess. After four or five samples, the gas would come out clear.

We fired up the motors and took off out of McCook, always anticipating that they would quit at the worst possible moment. We were on pins and needles, but the Shrike just hummed along as if nothing was wrong.

Jim had the autopilot on as I kept track of our location relatives to airports that we could use in an emergency.

The next stop was Peoria, Illinois, a little over six hundred miles away. We were losing daylight as we traveled east away from the sun.

It was late afternoon when we dropped into General Wayne Downing Airport. Peoria was far from the busy hustle of airspace around Chicago's O'Hare Airport.

We repeated the same routine from the last two days: always checking the fuel, and always being disappointed.

We were still eight hundred miles from Reading, and it was obvious we wouldn't make it before dark. However, Columbus, Ohio was about half that, so we decided we would stop there for the night.

With six hours and twelve minutes of flight time since leaving Colorado, it was dusk when we landed in Columbus and taxied to an FBO that Jim liked to use. Both of us breathed sighs of relief that the engines had kept running.

We locked the doors of the Shrike and a courtesy car drove us to a big hotel in the middle of the airport.

Not having eaten since the donuts and coffee that morning, we dropped our bags in our rooms and headed straight to the restaurant for a much-needed dinner, as well as a few beers for me and some kind of mixed drink for Jim.

Lying in the hotel bed, I pondered where I was and what I was doing. Halfway across the country, flying a sick airplane, or at least one with sick fuel, trying to get to an airshow because the aircraft was needed there. Risking my life along with Jim to get the job done. What was I thinking?

It didn't take long to realize; I was no stranger to risk and wouldn't have it any other way. I rolled over and went to sleep.

The next morning, we took time to get breakfast at the hotel. The courtesy car from the FBO dropped us off at the Shrike at eight-thirty. When the fuel truck arrived, the excited young man jumped out and said, "Hey, isn't this Bob Hoover's Aero Commander?"

Jim said, "Yeah, we're taking it to the Reading Airshow for him."

The fueler said, "Wow, I saw him fly in Dayton last year. He's incredible. What an honor to get to gas up his airplane."

Jim said, "What's your name? We'll tell him about you."

"Really? Holy cow, thanks. My name is Doug."

That was the reputation of Bob Hoover. Everyone in the flying world thought he was a superstar.

Once again, we were granted VFR weather in order to get to Reading. We took off to the east and climbed out over the lush green terrain of the Midwest. It was an area I hadn't flown over before. I kept thinking that it was beautiful country back here. I'd spent so much of my life in the West.

The gas had still been dirty when we checked it in Columbus. We continued holding our breaths as we flew eastward.

In just a little over two hours, we touched down at the Reading Regional Airport along the banks of the Schuylkill River on the northwest side of town. We were in time for Bob to do his demonstration that day – after he checked out the airplane, of course.

The first thing he did was drain the wing tank sump and view the Italian salad dressing gunk in the gas. Like we'd been doing, he pulled several samples. It started to come out cleaner, but not clean.

It was a testament to the durability of those Lycoming IO-540 engines. I'm still amazed that the fuel filters never clogged with that sludge.

As soon as Jim and I put our bags in a rental car, Bob hopped in the Shrike, fired up the motors, and got clearance from ground control to the active runway. Soon, he was disappearing to the west of the airport.

In twenty minutes, he was back. Shutting down and setting the parking brake, he climbed out and was draining the sump into the sampling jar as we walked up.

He said, "I wrung her out pretty good. No engine problems. Let's see how this looks."

The fuel sample came out as dirty as ever. We all sighed unhappily.

Being a test pilot for Rockwell he had intimate knowledge of the Shrike and it's systems. Bob explained, "The Shrike has one big tank in the spar that stretches across both wings. There is a rubber bladder that fits into the ribs of the wings, so there are a hundred places for that water and dirt to hide."

Jim asked, "Are you going to fly it this way?"

In his relaxed southern drawl he said, "I think it'll be okay. I'll never be far from the runway, and it's unlikely that both engines would quit at the same time."

The Reading Airshow was really an aviation industry trade show. The actual airshow demonstrations didn't start until five-thirty in the afternoon and continued for a little over an hour.

This year, the headliners were Wayne Pierce with his Stearman biplane and a pretty young lady as a wing walker, German Luftwaffe triple ace Oscar Boesch doing an aerobatic demonstration in a sailplane, the Canadian Reds in their Pitts P-2A biplanes, Bob Hoover, and, finally, the Thunderbirds.

Rockwell International, which was Bob's sponsor at the time, had set up a large tent in the vendor's area. While Bob was getting squared away with the Shrike, Jim took me over to the Rockwell tent and got us our identification badges so that we could go into restricted areas of the airport.

My badge said "Rockwell Pavilion" and, in big, bold numbers, "1980." I wore it proudly. Later that day, I was in the big tent with Bob and Jim when executives of Rockwell, including CEO Robert Anderson, came up to Bob to shake his hand and chat with him. Everywhere he went, he was the star of the aviation world.

Every time someone came up to say hello, if I happened to be standing near him, Bob, like the perfect gentleman he was, would introduce me to them, and they would act like they were very pleased to meet me. I suppose they figured that if I was with Bob, I was important. It felt very strange.

When it was time for his routine, Bob jumped in the Mustang and wowed the crowd like he always did. One little trick he liked to do at Reading was to dive out of view over the Schuylkill River, which was about sixty feet below the level of the airport.

He'd stay down there for about a quarter of a mile; you could hear a collective gasp and sudden silence from the crowd. Then he'd come rocketing back into view going almost straight up on the other side of the airport. Jim of course narrated the drama for full effect.

I was in my now-normal job of assisting Jim in his narration of the show, spotting Bob's location and direction as the P-51 roared back and forth, performing maneuvers and sometimes disappearing into the hazy East Coast sky as he climbed and turned to set up for his next pass.

When it came time to fly the Shrike, he didn't have the fuel drained and replaced. He figured if it had kept running this long, it might be okay.

Jim and I were on pins and needles during the first performance with the dirty gas. Almost no one else knew about it. However, Bob had already taken it up and "wrung it out," and he felt pretty confident that it would be alright.

If something did go wrong, there was no one better to be at the controls.

He did two shows, one with each airplane on Wednesday and Thursday. The Shrike's engines never so much as sputtered, let alone quit, but every time he landed and we checked the fuel, it looked as bad as ever.

Chapter 23
Reading, Pennsylvania

Inspiration and Perspiration

One evening, at a bar in the hotel where we were staying, Bob was the center of attention, as usual, when Jim told Bob about the pheasant in Nebraska and the runway light in Colorado.

Having been a fighter pilot in World War II, Bob laughed and said, "We need to paint those kills on the side of the Shrike, and we need to add a rattlesnake."

Someone in the crowd queried, "A rattlesnake?"

That gave Bob the cue to launch into another story.

"Yeah, ya see, a couple of years ago at Brown Field near San Diego, the line boy refueled the Shrike with jet fuel. Just after takeoff, at three hundred feet, I had just turned north when both engines quit. I was giving two folks a ride to Palomar, and I think about then they were wishing they'd made other plans. We were already away from the airport, and getting back to the runway was out of the question. I had to stick the nose down into a canyon, trying to find a place to make a crash landing. Once we got in this ravine, we found ourselves going uphill and the airspeed got slower and slower. Near the top, there was a flat spot, so I headed for it and pancaked the airplane into the hillside just below that little shelf. Going uphill, we slowed nicely. Just before we stopped, the Shrike came over the crest and plopped down in that clearing. I shut everything down and my passengers and I got out. We were all hobbling around with banged-up shins when I looked down. There, under the airplane, was a freshly deceased rattlesnake. I declared to my passengers, 'We have a casualty'!"

He embellished the last phrase as a punch line and the small crowd burst into laughter.

It would have been fun to have the three kills painted on the side of the airplane. I'd been present for two of them, but I don't think they ever did.

The time at Reading went by like a blur. So much was going on all the time, at the airport and then at the bar in the evening.

Friday afternoon, when the last airshow was over, the airport opened back up and aircraft started departing. Something had to be done with the Shrike. Though it had kept running, the gas just wouldn't clear up and Bob was concerned about continuing to fly it.

Jim told me, "Bob and I have decided the best thing to do is to take the Shrike to the factory in Oklahoma City where it was made. There, they can drain all of the fuel, take out the rubber fuel bladders, and wipe them down by hand with lint-free cloths. The FBO that put that dirty gas in there will be paying for it. It's going to take several weeks, so Bob will have to do the rest of the shows on his schedule with just the Mustang."

"Where will you be going?"

"I'll fly commercial to the next shows so I can do the narration, but I doubt that you can afford to do that."

Sadly, I said, "Yeah, you're right. I guess I'll have to fly home."

We left the rental car at the Rockwell Pavilion and threw our bags into the Shrike.

Bob came over and said, "You two have a safe trip, and remember, no night or IFR."

Jim said, "Don't worry about us, we'll be fine. I think we'll just go as far as Columbus tonight. Hey, we should get a picture."

I dug my camera out of my bag and handed it to someone from the small group that had followed Bob over. The three of us lined up in front of the Shrike.

Bob surprised me when he put his hand on my shoulder and pulled me against him like we'd been friends forever.

After saying our goodbyes, Jim and I flew off into the afternoon sun. We climbed to ten thousand feet on an IFR flight plan; I hand flew as much as possible, glancing out at the carpet of green that seemed to be everywhere east of the Mississippi River.

The engines on the Shrike purred along as if nothing was wrong. It was easy to get complacent, but we kept on our toes, noting the locations of airports along our route of flight, just in case.

Under two hours later, we had a great view of the orange, blue and green panorama ahead of us as the sun set into the hazy western sky. We were on the final approach to Columbus's runway Two Eight Left.

Jim and I had a nice dinner at the hotel restaurant right there at the airport. It was a quiet meal for a change, without the ever-present fan club around Bob.

Saturday morning, June 14, after breakfast at the hotel, we were in the air by nine o'clock, heading for Alton, Illinois for gas. Still forsaking the autopilot, I hand flew more than normal, with the feeling that this would be the last time.

After five hours and twelve minutes of flight time, we touched down at Oklahoma City's Downtown airport, just south of the Oklahoma River, We rolled out on the runway with the big buildings of the city in the distance.

As we unloaded our bags from the Shrike and into a courtesy car, I silently bade the airplane farewell, hoping that I would get to fly her again someday.

Soon, Jim and I were getting dropped off at Will Rogers Airport and it was time to say goodbye. It had been only ten days since I'd met Jim at Los Angeles Airport.

Standing on the sidewalk outside the terminal, we were about to head for different airlines. Jim said, "You look a little glum, champ. What's up?"

"I'm just sorry this is over. I've had such a great time."

Jim chuckled and said, "It's not over. We just have an interruption until we can fix that sick bird. You're welcome to come and travel with us again anytime when we get back to normal."

Then he added, with a smile, "As long as you can pay your way."

Laughing, I said, "Thanks, I'd like that. I'll be in touch."

I turned and walked off toward the Western Airlines terminal. My brush with greatness was over for now.

Bob, Dale, and Jim at Reading, PA. June 1980.

Epilogue
"This Too Shall Pass"

Months later, I saw Bob and Jim at airshows in California. Immediately, I was put back into my old job of being Jim's eyes during Bob's routine.

The Shrike had spent a month at the factory and was now back to normal. He was putting it through its paces just like he'd done with the dirty water in the fuel, as if nothing had been wrong.

At one of the airshows, I brought the photo of us together in Reading and they both signed it.

They treated me like an old friend. It was an honor, but life and my flying career got in the way. I never traveled with them or flew the Shrike again. Jim and I stayed in touch for years as I kept him updated on my flying career.

Bob Hoover is gone now and the aviation world seems emptier without him.

The Shrike, N500RA, is in the Smithsonian Air and Space Museum outside Washington DC. It sits under the left wing of an Air France Concorde. Nearby is a bronze statue of Bob Hoover, waving to the crowd with his Panama hat, just like he did after every airshow performance.

He was much more than simply the world's best pilot. His exploits during World War II are legendary, as is his work as a test pilot. He was an American hero and a true gentleman.

Being at an airshow with Bob Hoover was like going to The Oscars with John Wayne. For those ten days, it was as if I'd run away from home and joined the circus.

He was gracious and humble, and everyone was in awe of him. Every time I was near him, when someone came up to shake his hand, whether it was the president of Rockwell International or the Air Force Thunderbirds, he'd introduce me also, and they would respond as if I was somebody.

But I was a nobody. Bob didn't care. I think everybody was somebody to him. Especially if you were a pilot.

All of this happened because of a prop-bearing failure on a dark night in Nebraska the previous fall.

Though I never flew with him, just being around Bob Hoover and watching him fly over and over gave me a huge boost of inspiration and confidence to be a better pilot.

If he could do the extraordinary things he did with airplanes, then certainly I could do normal things.

I already was commercial, multi-engine, and instrument rated. It was only a matter of time before I would get hired as a pilot.

Look for the rest of that story and others in "Better Lucky Than Good, Book Two."

To Be Continued…

Excerpt from "Better Lucky Than Good, Book Two"

"Be careful what you wish for."

~Unknown

"Santa Rosa Tower, Air Attack four four zero is five miles east inbound with information Zulu."

"Roger Air Attack four four zero, proceed inbound, runway two-zero is recommended, but you can have whatever you need."

Information Zulu said the airport was closed. "Emergency in Progress." But it wasn't closed for us.

We were the emergency!

Circling the Santa Rosa airport at one thousand feet, Ranger Watson and I were in trouble. The O-2's landing gear was stuck halfway down.

Returning from a false alarm at our base at Columbia over an hour ago, the wheels wouldn't extend before landing.

Now at Santa Rosa, I had already made a couple of low passes down the runway so the maintenance people could see the problem.

We had plenty of gas, so we circled to burn off fuel, we didn't want to feed a fire if things didn't go well.

The Air Attack base at Columbia had called Sis-Q Flying Service on the phone to ask what they would like us to do. The answer was, "Bring it to company headquarters."

An hour later we arrived at the Sonoma Air Attack Base in Santa Rosa, fifty-five miles north of San Francisco. They were waiting for us, including all of the fire trucks at the airport.

On the flight over I had tried the emergency procedure several times which consisted of pumping a small handle on the floor connected to a hydraulic pump to operate the landing gear in whatever direction the gear selector was positioned. In this case, the handle was down. The procedure hadn't worked.

At some point we were going to have to land, wheels or no wheels. The fuel would only last so long and it was late in the afternoon, about six. We didn't want to do this in the dark.

An example of the trailing gear on an O-2/337.

With the landing gear hanging down, trailing back in the breeze, I wasn't confident about landing with it in such a position. Fearing it would tip the airplane on its side where a wingtip would dig in, we could cartwheel and roll up into a ball.

The possibility of fire was very real. I didn't tell this to Jerry Watson, but I gave him a briefing on what to expect.

"I'm not sure what will happen when we touch down, but when the airplane comes to a stop, get yourself out as quickly as possible. Don't worry about me, if I can't get out, that's what the rescue crews are here for."

Jerry's expression was grim, he just nodded. He wasn't having fun.

Aviation Glossary

ADF: Automatic direction finding, which, in the cockpit, consists of a dial pointing a needle that homes to a ground-based station known as an NDB, meaning non-directional beacon. It's the oldest air navigation system still in use today. (See NDB below.)

Airspeed: There are four kinds of airspeed.

Airspeed in miles per hour.

Airspeed in knots, or nautical miles per hour.

Indicated airspeed, which is what is read on the instrument panel. It's what the airplane thinks it's doing.

True airspeed, which is the real speed corrected for the thinner air at altitude and the temperature. "Relative to the air mass through which it's flying."

Then there's ground speed, the actual speed (miles per hour, or knots) over the ground depending on things such as air density and headwinds or tailwinds.

If you're flying a small airplane with an airspeed of one hundred miles per hour with a fifty-mile-per-hour tailwind, you have a ground speed of one hundred and fifty.

If you make a U-turn into that fifty-mile-per-hour wind (now a headwind), your ground speed will be fifty miles per hour. The cars on the interstate will be passing you.

Altitude: There are two kinds of altitude.

MSL, or above mean sea level, which needs to be corrected for pressure altitude with an altimeter setting in inches of mercury, adjusted for temperature.

AGL, or above ground level. That's important to keep you from hitting things.

ATC: Air traffic control. This a service provided by the FAA to direct aircraft through sections of controlled airspace and provide advisory services to aircraft in uncontrolled airspace. The primary purpose of ATC is to prevent collisions, organize and expedite the flow of air traffic, and provide information and other support for pilots.

Carburetor Heat: A system to put warm air into the carburetor to eliminate or prevent ice from building up in the fuel/air mixture as it accelerates through the venturi. Ice in the carburetor can cause the engine to stop running. Pilots hate that!

CFI – CFII: Certificated Flight Instructor. An already commercially rated pilot who has been licensed by the FAA to teach people to fly. The **II** designation means he/she is qualified to teach the much more complex instrument flying.

Some people will say "Certified" instead of "Certificated." A long time ago, an instructor stressed to me, "You have a certificate, you're certificated! Meat is certified!"

FAA: Federal Aviation Administration. The government agency that controls EVERYTHING related to airplanes and the sky over the United States. It also coordinates with the military and foreign governments.

FBO: Fixed base operator. A business that caters to pilots and their airplanes, selling gas, working on planes, and offering practically anything you might need.

FSS: Flight service station. Operated by the FAA, they provide information and services to pilots before, during, and after flights. Unlike air traffic control, they are not responsible for giving instructions or clearances or providing traffic separation. They do, however, relay clearances from ATC for departures and approaches. They are an important source of weather briefings for pilots.

Ground Loop: Wikipedia describes it as a rapid rotation of a fixed-wing aircraft in a horizontal plane (yawing) while on the ground that might cause the outside wing to touch the ground. In severe cases, the wing can dig in, causing the aircraft to swing violently or even cartwheel.

IFR: Instrument flight rules. Flying by instruments is primary, while looking out the window is secondary. IFR flight is regulated by the FAA with a gazillion rules and regulations. Procedures and training are significantly more complex compared to VFR instruction. Pilots must demonstrate competency in conducting an entire cross-country flight and approach to landing solely by reference to instruments. Commercial airliners operate under IFR flight plans on every flight. Not only must a pilot be licensed to fly IFR, but he or she also must be current within the previous 90 days. The aircraft must be properly equipped for IFR flight operations and must have been recently inspected to qualify.

ILS: Instrument landing system. A precision radio navigation system that allows pilots to find a runway through clouds or other reduced visibility conditions. Because it's so precise, commercial pilots use this method constantly, even in good weather when the runway is plainly visible. The ILS provides both vertical and horizontal radio beams, displayed as crossed needles in the cockpit, that guide the aircraft to the touchdown zone of a runway. A pilot needs special training to perform this maneuver without being able to see outside. Hardest of all is doing it in a multi-engine airplane with one or more engines inoperative. Modern jets can land themselves on autopilot.

Mixture Control: A knob next to the throttle that controls the fuel/air ratio (mixture) in the carburetor. Used at higher altitudes to reduc,e the amount of fuel to compensate for lower air density. Rich for more fuel ratio, lean for less. Normally set at full rich for takeoff.

NDB: A non-directional beacon is a ground station that puts out a signal that can be used for navigation or approaches by the pilot using the

ADF radio in an airplane. Simple but effective. They are not very precise, but even today most airports still have NDB approaches so that pilots can land in IFR conditions. IFR pilots must prove competency on initial check rides and requalifying check rides.

Propeller: A big fan that keeps the pilot cool. Turn it off and watch him/her sweat.

Sectional Chart: A local chart at 1:500,000 scale made for VFR pilots to navigate visually. They provide all navigation aids and topographical information to navigate visually. Checkpoints include populated areas, drainage patterns, roads, railroads, and other distinctive landmarks. Also included are airports, controlled airspace, restricted areas, and obstructions.

Stall: In aerodynamics, a stall refers to the airflow **over** the wing and has nothing to do with the engine. It's the wing that holds the airplane up. The engine only propels it forward to provide that lift. If the wing stalls, the airplane will fall. With enough altitude, you can point the nose down and get it flying again. With not enough altitude, you will hit the ground. Basic physics will get you every time. Larger, faster airplanes need a lot more altitude to recover than do smaller, slower airplanes.

Tarmac: A British word meaning the combination of tar and macadam. In America, we call it asphalt.

TCA: Terminal control area. The airspace around large airports. Normally, it is very busy airspace with many commercial aircraft coming and going. Usually jets. Radio contact with air traffic control is mandatory.

Tower: An air traffic control tower at an airport controls operations on and around the airport, including ground operations, usually on a separate radio frequency. Contact and participation are mandatory unless prior authorization is obtained for a Nordo (No Radio) aircraft. It's also possible to get coded light signals from the tower. Knowing what they mean is part of your training.

VFR: Visual flight rules. Simpler than IFR, looking out the window is primary, while using instruments for orientation (staying right-side-up) and navigation (getting where you're going) is secondary. With my little Cessna 140, they were not required. VFR flying is easier and more fun.

VHF: Very high frequency radio.

VOR: VHF omnidirectional range. This means a radial beam for every point of the compass, 360 degrees. You can determine your exact bearing from a station, track it inbound or outbound, or identify intersections from crossing radials of other VOR stations. It's very precise compared to ADF/NDB navigation.

WAC: World Aeronautical Chart. Also for VFR navigation, WACs have half the detail of sectional charts, but cover much more territory. They have a scale of 1:1,000,000, which is about 1 inch = 13.7 nautical miles or 16 statute miles. Twelve WACs will cover the continental United States.

Wet Compass: Sometimes called a whisky compass because the early ones floated in alcohol. Newer ones use kerosene. They bounce around and are not very accurate, but in a pinch, they are better than nothing.

Also by this author:

Dale Arenson
HANGMEN
Riding with an Outlaw Motorcycle Club in the old days.

Reviews for "Hangmen" on Amazon

*It's multidimensional, entertaining,
and inspiring as well as informational.*

~Yaeko G.

*Quite a good story and told in a very down to earth way.
The author is quite eloquent.*

~Keith O.

I only wish he would write more. Seriously, this man has a gift.

~Vic

*Could not put it down, great writing style,
easy to follow and really puts you in the action. Brilliant.*

~Graeme G.

Wow! I cried when this book ended because I enjoyed it so much.

~Janne B.

*The thing I enjoyed most was the honesty about the biker world.
Better than Hunter Thompson's book.*

~Appleton

He tells a hell of a story in an extremely well written style.

~S. Storter

*Filled with excitement, comedy, and emotional drama.
My only complaint is that it left me wanting more.*

~Tia O.

*An amazing history told in an exciting way.
Thoroughly enjoyed this book. I'm amazed at the life he lived.*

~Syndi C.

I can't say enough great things about this book.

~Hurley

*An exciting fun book to burn through, with an unusual ending.
He survives.*

~Matt

Loved the book. Sorry to see it end! Waiting for more.

~Melodee U.

*The ending is wonderful and very sweet,
and I was happy to learn how it ended.*

~Chris R.

*I didn't want this book to end. Such a carefree life
and memoirs with such a great memory. I felt like
I was riding along with him much of the time. What a fun find.*

~Rami C.

*Dale goes through gut wrenching situations that would leave most
people with nightmare[s] for the rest of their lives. Great book.*

~Kris R.

Dale Arenson

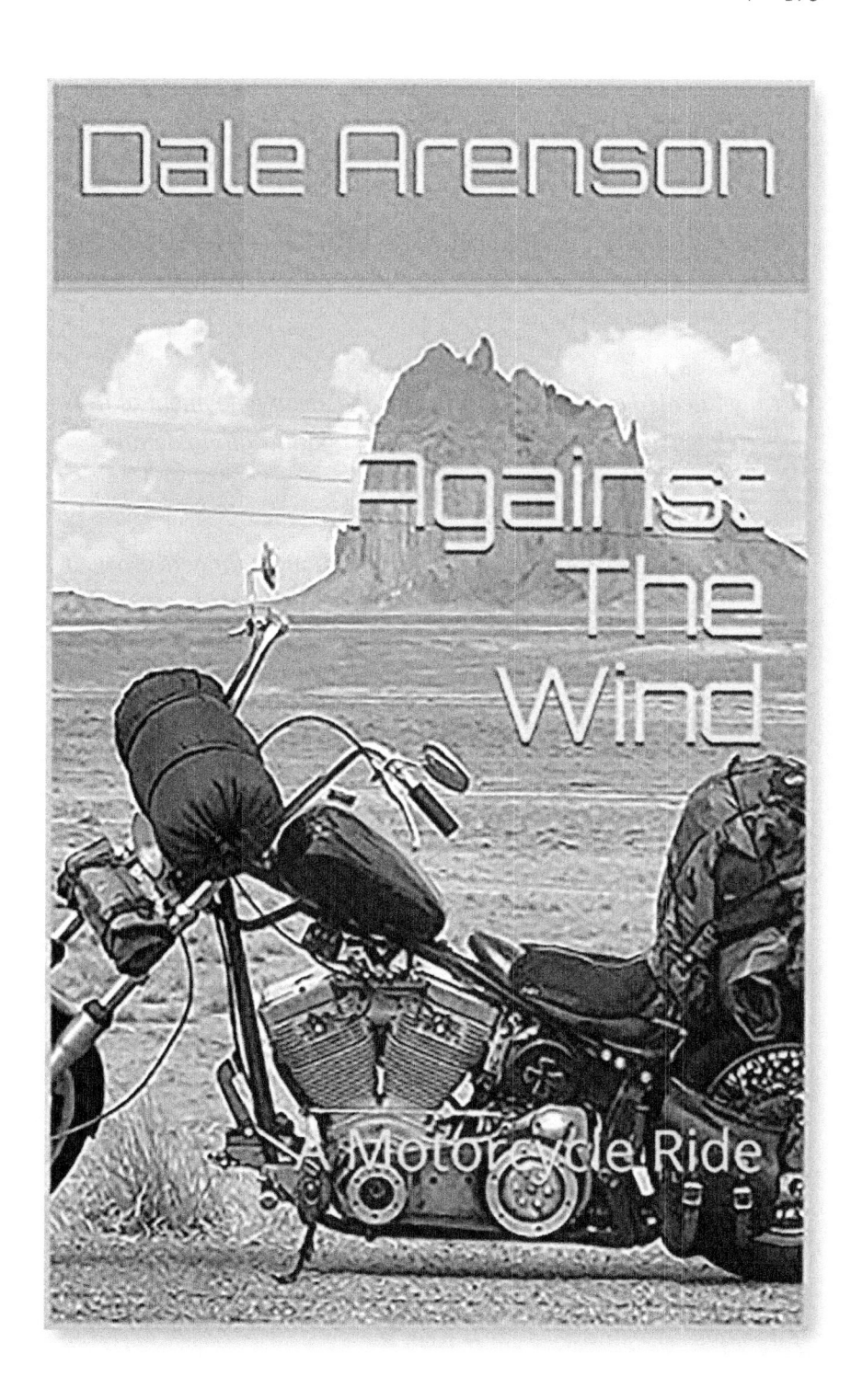

Against The Wind

A Motorcycle Ride

Reviews for "Against the Wind" on Amazon

A truly talented storyteller, writing for the sheer enjoyment of it. He relates his life experiences in vivid and intriguing detail.

~ Chris V.

Really easy read, kept me hooked right through. Fingers crossed this guy writes more stuff. Priceless!

~ Chris H.

Reading this book sure made me want to go out and jump on a motorcycle and ride for some time.

~ Dennis O.

He even throws in a good dose of humor and philosophy in his narrative as well as historical and other factual information, making it such a rich read.

~ Yaeko G.

Love reading his clear and concise writing. Dale has a way of writing that constructs vivid mental pictures. Highly recommended and worth reading.

~ Janne B.

Even after 50 years, you can still live your dreams.

~ Kris R.

My deepest appreciation to everyone who takes the time to leave a written review on Amazon, Barnes & Noble, or Goodreads.

You can contact the author at his website,
dalearenson.com,
Email dale@dalearenson.com,
or on Facebook.